BREAKING
Intimidation

JOHN BEVERE
AUTHOR OF *The Bait of Satan*

CREATION
HOUSE
BOOKS ABOUT SPIRIT-LED LIVING
ORLANDO, FLORIDA

BREAKING INTIMIDATION by John Bevere
Published by Creation House
Strang Communications Company
600 Rinehart Road
Lake Mary, FL 32746
Web site: http://www.creationhouse.com

Unless otherwise noted, all Scripture quotations are from the New King James Version of the Bible. Copyright © 1979, 1980, 1982 by Thomas Nelson, Inc., publishers. Used by permission.

Scripture quotations marked AMP are from the Amplified Bible. Old Testament copyright © 1965, 1987 by the Zondervan Corporation. The Amplified New Testament copyright © 1954, 1958, 1987 by the Lockman Foundation. Used by permission.

Scripture quotations marked KJV are from the King James Version of the Bible

Scripture quotations marked NIV are from the Holy Bible, New International Version. Copyright © 1973, 1978, 1984, International Bible Society. Used by permission.

Library of Congress Catalog Card Number: 94-73852
International Standard Book Number: 0-88419-387-X

8 9 0 1 2 3 4 5 BBG 14 13 12 11 10 9
Printed in the United States of America

My deepest appreciation to...

My wife, Lisa. Next to the Lord, you are my dearest friend.
I am eternally grateful to the Lord for the privilege of
being married to you. Thank you for the hours of editing
you contributed to this book. I love you, sweetheart!

To our four sons...
To Addison, I am grateful for your tender heart.
You live up to your name, "trustworthy."
To Austin, I am grateful for your
selfless love and sensitivity.
To Alexander, I love the way you light
up a room with your presence.
To Arden, you bring us tremendous joy.

To John and Kay Bevere, for being the godly parents
you are. I am so glad the Lord allowed me to be
your son. I love you both.

To the staff of John Bevere Ministries, thank you
for your support and faithfulness.

A special thanks to John Mason, a genuine friend,
who truly rejoices at the success of others.

To the entire Creation House staff who have labored
with us and been so supportive of our ministry. You all
are special partners and friends in the ministry.

Most important, my sincere gratitude to our Father
in heaven for His unfailing love, to our Lord Jesus
for His grace, truth and love, and to the Holy Spirit
for His faithful guidance during this project.

As I was writing this book, God spoke to me prophetically and said:

*There are many called to My great
end-time army of believers
who are bound by intimidation.
They have pure hearts toward God
and man; however, like Gideon of old,
they are held captive
by the fear of man (Judg. 6–8).
The gifts I placed in them are dormant.*

*I will anoint the message of this book
to liberate multitudes of them.
They will step out and fearlessly obey Me.
They shall be valiant warriors
and shall bring forth great victories
in the strength of their God.*

It has been my privilege to know John Bevere as a fellow minister and dear friend for many years. I believe with all my heart that God has raised him up to bring a message of victory, faith and hope to this generation.

In *Breaking Intimidation* John Bevere brings a timely, much needed message to the body of Christ. We need to use the gifts that God has given us to reach the world. But instead, many of us are backing down because of subtle and not-so-subtle attacks to our authority in Christ.

Satan will arrange circumstances and use people to stop the gift of God in you any way he can. The Word of God includes many examples of believers who were intimidated and broke through to victory — Joshua, Gideon, Nehemiah and David, to name just a few. The Bible says,

No weapon formed against you shall prosper
(Is. 54:17).

Through this book and the power of the Holy Spirit,
every believer can break through intimidation into victory.
May God raise up in this generation an army of warriors
who will never back down!

John Mason
Author of *An Enemy Called Average, Let Go of Whatever
Makes You Stop* and *Words of Promise*

Countless Christians battle intimidation, yet most wrestle with its effects rather than battling the source. Picture a lovely home with expensive furnishings, but with a section of the roof missing. A heavy rain comes and floods the entire house; most everything is ruined. It takes days to remove all the soiled and damaged furnishings, drapery and flooring. Then the owner diligently labors to replace all that was destroyed.

When his work is almost complete another storm destroys all his interior restoration. Frustrated, he begins again the tedious and discouraging job of restoration. It is only a matter of time before the rain destroys everything, and with every downpour his strength and resources are depleted. Discouraged, he eventually stops his work and settles for what he believes is his lot in life.

Of course, this sounds absurd. You're probably thinking, Why doesn't he fix the roof and then restore what was lost? What a silly person! However, this scenario describes how many battle with intimidation. They struggle to correct its effects — discouragement, confusion, hopelessness, despair and so on — rather than breaking the power of intimidation!

Some battle intimidation by going to counselors to learn how to function with their fears. Others resign themselves to a life of slavery to timidity, afraid to hope for freedom. Both of these are like living with a hole in your roof and soggy furniture. Others withdraw into isolation. Hopeless, they leave their soggy house altogether.

The message in this book will not teach you to cope. It will share God's way to freedom from all fear and intimidation. Then you can fulfill the call of God on your life.

I have spent many hours at my computer, working on this book and asking the Lord to guide me as I wrote. One morning as I was working I felt the presence of the Lord come into the room. I got up from the computer and began to walk and pray. As I prayed, the Spirit of the Lord came upon me to prophecy, and these words came forth:

> Son, there are many called to my great end-time army of believers who are bound by intimidation. They have pure hearts toward God and man; however, like Gideon of old, they are held captive by the fear of man (Judg. 6–8). The gifts I placed in them are dormant. I will anoint the message of this book to liberate multitudes of them. They will step out and fearlessly obey Me. They shall be valiant warriors and shall bring forth great victories in the strength of their God.

This is not just a theoretical teaching. For years I was

bound by intimidation. The biggest obstacle I faced was not knowing the source of my problems. God exposed this wicked enemy. Since then, God has used this message to liberate Christians all over the world.

One leader exclaimed, "This message needs to be in the hands of every pastor in America!" It is not a message only for the pastors but for everyone in the church. I do not believe it is an accident this book is in your hands. As you are liberated, please share this message with others who need it. Sharing it will strengthen the message in you.

I encourage you to join me in prayer as you begin your adventure. Please open your heart and speak these words in God's presence.

> Father, in the name of my Lord Jesus Christ, I ask the Holy Spirit to reveal Your Word to me as I read this book. Please expose and remove any insecurities in my life, so the very root of intimidation will be destroyed. May I draw closer to You and, with boldness, witness of my Lord Jesus Christ.

ESTABLISHING
YOUR SPIRITUAL POSITION

Walk in your God-given authority, or someone will take it and use it against you.

Chapter 1

WALK IN YOUR AUTHORITY

As I serve the Lord, I realize more and more that He uses circumstances and people to prepare us to fulfill His calling for our lives.

In 1983 I left my career position as an engineer to enter the full-time ministry of helps for a very large church. In my position I served the pastor, his wife and all incoming guest ministers by taking care of menial tasks in order to free them up for the work God called them to do. After four years God released me to be the youth pastor for another large church.

The week I was to leave, a man who was also on staff told my wife that God had given him a word for me. Ever since then that word has resounded in my ear as a warning, offering protection in the shadow of its wisdom and strength. As with any true word of God it has become a rudder for my heart and a foundation to keep me from uncertainty.

This man warned my wife, "If John does not walk in his God-given authority, someone will take it from him and use it against him." This word had an immediate impact. I recognized it as the wisdom of God, but I did not have the full understanding of how to apply it. That knowledge would come over the next several years.

A Life-changing Experience

At the beginning of 1990 the Lord confirmed that His calling on my life at that time was to travel and minister. After I had been on the road for a short time, I had a life-changing experience through which I finally understood the words of instruction God had given me years before.

We had begun conducting the meetings at a church on a Wednesday evening and were scheduled to continue through Sunday. The Spirit of God moved in a very powerful way, and there were strong deliverances, healings and salvation. The presence of God in the meetings grew each night.

The first week a lady involved in the New Age movement was gloriously delivered. This seemed to be the catalyst that spurred the meetings on. Within a week people were coming from a ninety-mile radius.

The pastor said, "We can't stop these meetings. God has more in store for us." I agreed, and we continued for twenty-one services. The Word of God flowed like a swift-running brook, and the gifts of the Spirit manifested in every service.

During the second week of the meetings, one night I turned around as I was preaching and faced the musicians and singers (there were about twenty-five on the platform).

Then I declared, "There is sin on this platform. If you do not repent, God will expose it."

After hearing myself say that, I thought, Wow, where did that come from? I had been preaching long enough to know there are times when God's anointing on you is so strong that you will make statements that your physical ears will hear only after they're already said. This is prophetic preaching — when we speak by divine inspiration.

My mind began to question what I said, but I quickly dismissed those thoughts because I knew what I said was from God. I had not premeditated it. The anointing to preach remained heavily upon me.

The crowds grew at each service. During the third week — again, as I preached — I wheeled around, pointed my finger at those on the platform and declared boldly through the unction of the Holy Spirit, "There is sin on this platform. If you do not repent, God will expose it, and you will be removed!" I sensed an increase in authority and assurance. This time I did not question it because I knew God was in the process of purging sin from His house.

Judge or Be Judged

If sin creeps into our lives, the Holy Spirit convicts and instructs us. However, if we do not listen, we will begin to grow cold and dull. This will continue until we are no longer sensitive to Him in our hearts.

Then, in order to reach and protect us or those around us, God will send someone to expose what is wrong. He does not do this for the purpose of embarrassing us but to warn and protect us. If we still refuse to listen, judgment comes. "For if we would judge ourselves, we would not be judged. But when we are judged, we are chastened by the Lord, that we may not be condemned with the world" (1 Cor. 11:31-32).

God will tolerate sin for a season to give us time to

repent in order to spare us His chastening. Even in His chastening it is His desire that we would not be condemned along with the world. The prodigal son came to his senses when he was in the pigpen. Better to come to your senses in a pigpen than to continue in your sin and one day hear the Master say, "Depart from Me, you who practice lawlessness" (Matt. 7:23)!

If we do not repent, we suffer even though that is not God's desire for us. Referring to this, Paul said, "For this reason many are weak and sick among you, and many sleep [are dead]" (1 Cor. 11:30). Sin eventually brings forth spiritual and physical death. I felt that the Lord was chastening someone on the platform, trying to bring that person to repentance. But I did not know whom He was convicting of sin.

A Subtle Attack of Intimidation

The next evening as the pastor and I were in his office preparing to go out to the service, an elder came in and reported that the ministers of music and praise seemed moody and negative that night. The pastor thought they were just tired from so many services and said, "Just tell them to go out and praise God and put their feelings aside."

I looked at the elder and said, "Wait a minute. Is there something wrong?"

The elder answered, "Well, they think you are being too hard on them. They feel that you should address them privately rather than publicly."

Although I was unaware of it at the time, this was a very crucial moment. My God-given authority to serve and protect was being challenged. The enemy was not pleased with what was happening in these meetings, and he wanted to put a stop to it.

I had a choice, although at that time I was not aware of it. I could yield to the intimidation by backing down on what I had said to the ministers of music, thereby forfeiting my position of authority. Or I could stay in my authority, breaking the power of their intimidation by staying strong in what God had said.

Immediately I thought, John, why did you embarrass those people? Why couldn't you just preach your message without turning around and pointing fingers? Now the people in the church are busy trying to figure out who on the platform is in sin. What if no one is? Or even if there is sin, what if it's never exposed? People will still be suspicious, and those who are pure will suffer. The church will be hindered. Have I destroyed the good that has been done in this church? If I have, it will give me a bad reputation, and I've only just started to travel.

On and on these thoughts assaulted my mind. My fears had begun to center on one thought: What is going to happen to me? This is how intimidation will change your focus. The reason: The root of intimidation is fear, and fear causes people to focus on themselves. Perfect love casts out fear because love puts the focus on God and others and denies itself (1 John 4:18).

The pastor said nothing. The three of us grabbed hands and prayed that God's will would be done in that service. We proceeded out to the platform just as we had each night for the past three weeks. During the praise and worship I noticed the word of the Lord was not filling my heart. I felt no direction, but I thought, God is faithful. I'll know what to say and do by the time I get to the pulpit.

Praise and worship was over, and as the pastor made announcements, I heard nothing in my heart. I thought, I'll get up and God will give me direction as I stand on my feet. I am not one who prepares outlines and has sermons ready. I study, pray and then speak from my heart by inspiration. My concern grew as the time passed because I knew I had nothing to say if God did not give me His direction.

Then the pastor introduced me. I came to the pulpit, and because I had no direction, I said, "Let's pray." But as we prayed, I still received no direction. I prayed for several minutes. To make matters worse my prayers were lifeless. It was as if my words were coming out of my mouth only to fall at my feet. I thought, What am I going to do? I resolved to deliver a message out of the Psalms that I had preached before.

As I preached, I sensed no life, no anointing on the message. I struggled to keep my thoughts together. God seemed nowhere to be found. I would think, Why did I just say that? or, Where am I taking this? It was as if I were being led by confusion, not by the Holy Spirit. I kept consoling myself that God would show up and salvage the mess I was in. However, it just got worse. I finally ended the message and the service after about thirty-five minutes.

Baffled, I went back to the place where I was staying. "God, why didn't You show up?" I asked. "Every service has been wonderful and powerful, yet this service had no life. If I were the people, I wouldn't come back. As a matter of fact, I don't want to go back." That night I went to bed feeling as if I'd swallowed a sack of sand.

The next morning I woke up feeling as if the sack of sand had grown into a pile. I felt so heavy that I didn't want to get out of bed. Joy eluded me. I went out to pray. I asked God again, "Why didn't You show up?"

No response.

"Have I sinned? Did I grieve You?"

Still silence. I prayed for an hour, and every minute was a struggle.

I put on a praise tape and began to sing along. I reasoned, God gives the garment of praise for the spirit of heaviness. I have got to get rid of this. However, I only experienced a half hour of lifeless singing. I became more frustrated. "What have I done? Why won't You answer me?"

After lunch I went out to a nearby field. I thought, I'll bind the devil. That will do it. But I was the only one who felt bound. I was out praying and yelling at the devil for three hours and almost lost my voice. I had to go in and get ready for the service. I consoled myself: With all this resistance, tonight God will show up strong. John, just walk by faith.

We went through the praise, worship, announcements and offering that night, and I felt the same foreboding I had the night before. Again I reasoned, God will come through as soon as I get up there. I was introduced and again — nothing. I prayed for direction, and there was silence.

I began to preach another message I had ministered before and was overwhelmed with confusion. There was no life, direction or anointing. After five minutes of this mess I said, "Folks, we need to pray. Something is just not right!" The entire congregation stood up, and we all began to pray fervently.

Intimidation Exposed

All of a sudden I heard the voice of God speak to me for the first time in more than twenty-four hours. He said, "John, you are intimidated by those people on the platform behind you. You've been knocked out of your position of authority, and the gift of God in you has been quenched."

With this gentle rebuke a burst of light flooded my spirit. While everyone prayed for the next five minutes, the Spirit of God walked me through the Bible, showing me numerous incidents when men and women were intimidated and how this caused the gift of God in them to go dormant. I saw how they yielded their authority and lost their effectiveness in the Spirit. Then He walked me through the past several years and showed me how I'd done the same.

I immediately began breaking the power of intimidation

off myself through prayer. There's an example of this kind of prayer in the epilogue. For the next seventy-five minutes I preached from the Scriptures God had given me like a man on fire. When I finished, two-thirds of the congregation came forward to receive freedom from intimidation. That was the greatest service of the entire revival.

Less than a week later God started to expose the sin on the platform. It was discovered that the bass player was going out after services and getting drunk. In addition one of the singers was sleeping with a young girl in the congregation. They were both removed from their ministry positions. The bass player left the church, but the singer repented and was restored in his walk with the Lord.

A short time later the praise and worship leader and a few others caused a split in the church. A fourth of the church left with them. As it turned out, the praise and worship leader was involved in adultery, and within a year she divorced her husband. At last report she was living with another man. Out of the families that led the split, only one couple is still married.

These were the people who had complained that I was too hard on them. God was giving them a warning. How much better it would have been if only they had taken that warning to heart.

I have returned to this church twice and discovered more unity and strength there than ever before. The pastor explained, "It was God purging our church, and it has made us stronger. Our praise and worship has never been so free!" He also said a lot of the contention and strife he'd previously dealt with was no longer there. Praise God!

What God imparted in that short five minutes of prayer during that service has grown into the message you are about to read. He has led me to preach this message all over the world. As a result, I have seen countless men and women liberated from the captivity of intimidation.

A Message for All

Although this message was revealed as I sought God in the midst of a ministry conflict, do not think its lesson is limited to those who stand behind a pulpit. Countless Christians battle intimidation. Often those who are intimidated don't realize what they're fighting. As with most of Satan's devices, intimidation is camouflaged and subtle. We feel its effects — depression, confusion, lack of faith — without knowing its root. Had I realized I was intimidated, I would not have had such a struggle at that church. But I thank God for the lesson it taught me.

In frustration most of us deal with the aftermath, or fruit, of intimidation rather than with intimidation itself — and with its root. Therefore, we may experience temporary relief, but our struggles do not end. You can pick all the fruit off a tree, but as long as its roots are intact, the fruit eventually grows back. This cycle can be discouraging because we feel as though we just cannot rid ourselves of these hindrances. We begin to feel hopeless and settle for a place far below where God has called us.

The truths in this book will help you not only to identify intimidation but also to equip you with the knowledge you need to break its hold on your life. It is my prayer that as you read and walk in these truths, you will be liberated to fulfill your call as a servant of our Lord Jesus Christ.

You may now be anxious to confront the intimidation in your life head on. Often when we see something in our lives that has oppressed us we want immediate relief, but usually the immediate fix comes with a high price: It is not permanent. I want to unfold carefully this message as it was revealed to me. In the next three chapters I will lay a crucial foundation, starting with understanding our spiritual position and authority.

21

Satan seeks to displace us in order to regain the authority Jesus stripped from him.

Chapter 2

SPIRITUAL
POSITION AND AUTHORITY

L et's begin by discussing the word given to me: If you don't walk in your God-given authority, someone will take it from you and use it against you.

First, it is important to understand there is a dwelling place or position in the spirit that we hold as believers in Jesus. With this position comes authority. This authority is what the enemy wants. If he can get us to yield our God-given authority, he will take it and use it against us. This not only affects us but also those entrusted to our care.

There are several scriptures pertaining to our place of authority in the spirit. Let's examine a few.

> He who dwells in the secret place of the Most High shall abide under the shadow of the

Almighty (Ps. 91:1).

He also brought me out into a broad place;
He delivered me because He delighted in me
(Ps. 18:19).

My foot stands in an even place; in the congregations I will bless the Lord (Ps. 26:12).

Believers literally occupy a *place* in the spirit. It is
imperative that you as a believer not only know that place
but also function in it. If you do not know your position,
you cannot function properly in the body of Christ.

This position and the authority it carries can be lost or
stolen. A clear biblical example is Judas Iscariot. After
Jesus ascended to heaven, the disciples gathered to pray.
At that time, Peter explained what had happened to Judas:

For it is written in the book of Psalms: "Let his
dwelling place be desolate, and let no one live
in it" (Acts 1:20).

Judas permanently lost his place in the spirit by transgression (Acts 1:16-17). This is the primary way the enemy
knocks people out of their spiritual authority. It is how he
caused Adam and Eve to fall, consequently displacing
them and gaining lordship over them and all they ruled.

Adam and Eve held the highest position of authority on
the earth. Every living creature and all of nature were
under their authority. God said, "Let them have dominion
over the fish of the sea, over the birds of the air, and over
the cattle, over all the earth and over every creeping thing
that creeps on the earth" (Gen. 1:26). Nothing on this
earth in the spiritual or natural realms was above the
authority of mankind — only God Himself.

When Adam held his position of authority, there was
no disease, earthquakes, famine or poverty. It was the
dominion of heaven on this earth as Adam walked in

fellowship with God and ruled by God's delegated authority and power. But with the sin of Adam came the demise of everything underneath his authority. By transgression he yielded his place in the spirit to the enemy of God.

The Scriptures bear testimony to this by Satan's boast as he tempted Jesus in the wilderness. Satan took Him on a high mountain to show Him all the kingdoms of the world, declaring:

> All this authority I will give You, and their glory;
> for this has been delivered to me, and I give it to
> whomever I wish (Luke 4:6).

God had entrusted authority to Adam, and Adam in turn forfeited it to Satan. Adam lost more than just his position. *All* that God had placed under his care was affected. A gradual decline of all harmony and order took place.

One example is in the animal kingdom. In the garden, under God and Adam's domain, lions did not devour the other animals (Is. 65:25). Cobras did not have venomous bites (Is. 65:25). Lambs had no reason to fear wolves or other creatures of prey (Is. 65:25). Yet, immediately after the fall we see an innocent animal sacrificed to clothe the naked man (Gen. 3:21). Later we see enmity and fear placed between man and the animals that he once ruled over (Gen. 9:2)

Another area affected was the earth itself. The ground became cursed, working against man instead of for him as he toiled to bring forth the fruit that once had been bountifully provided (Gen. 3:17-19). Romans 8:20 tells us, "For the creation was subjected to futility, not willingly."

Nothing on earth, whether natural or spiritual, escaped the effects of disobedience. Iniquity, death, disease, poverty, earthquakes, famines, pestilence and more entered the earth. There was a loss of divine order and authority. Adam's firstborn learned to hate, envy and murder. The enemy had taken the authority God had given for protection and provision and turned it against all creation using it now for destruction and death.

Restored Authority

A man forfeited his position of authority; therefore, only a man could restore it. Thousands of years later Jesus was born. His mother was a daughter of God's covenant people; His Father, the Holy Spirit of God. He was not part man and part God. He was *Emmanuel,* "God revealed in a man" (Matt. 1:23). The fact that He was human gave Him the legal right to regain what was lost. Because He was the Son of God He was free from the lordship the enemy had acquired over man.

He revealed the will of God in everything He did and said. Sins were forgiven because in His presence sin had no dominion. Sickness and disease bowed to His authority and power (Luke 5:20-24). Nature itself was subjected to His command (Mark 4:4). He walked in the authority that Adam had relinquished. Jesus, through obedience and sacrifice, restored the God-given authority Adam had lost, and therefore, our relationship with God .

Before He returned to His Father, Jesus declared, "All authority has been given to Me in heaven and on earth. Go therefore and make disciples of all the nations, baptizing them in the name of the Father and of the Son and of the Holy Spirit, teaching them to observe all things that I have commanded you: and lo, I am with you always, even to the end of the age" (Matt. 28:18-20).

It is clear that Jesus regained what Adam lost and more. Satan and Adam only had dominion over the earth, but Jesus' dominion included not only the earth but also heaven.

Jesus had risen above the place of authority Satan had dispossessed. After revealing His position and authority, Jesus told us to "go therefore." Why did Jesus make this connection between His authority and our calling? We find the answer in the writings of the apostle Paul.

Positions of Authority

Paul prayed we would know "what is the exceeding greatness of His power toward us who believe...which He worked in Christ when He raised Him from the dead and seated Him at His right hand in the heavenly *places*" (Eph. 1:19-20). Notice it is not a singular heavenly place; Paul clearly says "places." The reason for this is found a few verses later as we read, "And you He made alive, who were dead in trespasses and sins...and raised us up together, and made us sit together in the heavenly *places* in Christ Jesus" (Eph. 2:2,6). These *places* are where His redeemed children are to dwell.

Now the question, Where are these dwelling places, and what position do they hold? The answer is found in Ephesians 1:21: "far *above* all principality and power and might and dominion, and every name that is named, not only in this age but also in that which is to come" (italics added).

A redeemed man hidden in Christ is now given a position in the spirit above the devil. Jesus boldly declared, "Behold, I give you the authority...over all the power of the enemy, and nothing shall by any means hurt you" (Luke 10:19).

Now we understand the command, "Go therefore." Jesus understood the authority He was entrusting to believers. Our rebirth rights have positioned us in those heavenly places far above the enemy's authority and power.

Just as he did with Adam in the Garden of Eden, Satan now seeks to displace us in the spirit in order to regain the authority Jesus stripped from him. If Satan can steal or cause individuals to lay down their position of authority, then he once again has authority to operate. Paul says so clearly, "[Do not] give *place* to the devil" (Eph. 4:27, italics added). We believers must not forfeit our place in the spirit.

Rank in the Kingdom

We must realize the kingdom of God is just that — a *kingdom*. Kingdoms are structured by rank and authority. Heaven's domain is no exception. The higher the rank, the more influence and authority.

In the garden, Satan wasn't after the elephant or even the lion. He understood authority and went after God's man. He knew if he got the man he would possess all that he ruled over and cared for.

So when the enemy goes after a church, his primary target is the leadership. Recently a pastor of a large congregation decided to divorce his wife. There was no scriptural reason for this, and it devastated his wife and children. When the leadership under him questioned his motive, he told them if they didn't like it they could leave.

He willfully transgressed the commandment of God, releasing a spirit of divorce and deception throughout his congregation. After this, there was an increase of divorce in his church, even among leadership. Others became discouraged. Shell-shocked, they drifted from church to church, wondering whom they could trust. When Satan knocks the *keeper of a house* out of his position, all those under his care are vulnerable.

I have watched as parents willfully transgress the commandments of God. It is then only a matter of time before their children follow their example. You may call it a curse, but why does it happen? Through sin parents have forfeited their position of authority in the spirit, leaving their children vulnerable to the enemy.

Giving Occasion to the Enemies of the Lord

This principle is illustrated in the life of David (2 Sam. 8-18). The kingdom was strong and secure under his leadership. God had blessed him with several sons and daughters. Then David took for himself what God had not given him; he committed adultery with Bathsheba. She became pregnant, and to complicate matters, her husband was away at war defending David's realm.

David sent for her husband, Uriah, hoping to encourage him to sleep with Bathsheba and therefore appear to have fathered the baby. However, Uriah, in devotion to David and his kingdom, would not enjoy intimacy with his wife while his fellow soldiers were in combat. David saw that the plan to cover his sin was not going to work. He knew it would only be a matter of time before Uriah learned his wife was pregnant. Eventually everyone would know the father was David.

So David planned Uriah's murder, sending him back to the battle carrying his own death warrant. Uriah was put amid the fiercest fighting. Then, when he was surrounded by the enemy, those fighting beside him were ordered to draw back. Uriah fell by the enemy's hand. David's one act of adultery led to deceit, lying and murder.

Soon the prophet Nathan came to David to expose this sin. David confessed, "I have sinned against the Lord." Then Nathan said to David, "The Lord also has put away your sin; you shall not die" (2 Sam. 12:13).

David repented and was forgiven. God released him from his transgression (Is. 43:25-26). But Nathan goes on to warn David: "By this deed you have given great occasion to the enemies of the Lord" (2 Sam. 12:14).

David was forgiven, but he had made his life and family vulnerable to the enemies of God — not only natural enemies but also spiritual ones. His family and the nation of Israel suffered greatly.

David's first child by Bathsheba died. David's oldest son, Amnon, heir to the throne, raped his half-sister, Tamar. Absalom, son of David and brother of Tamar, took revenge and killed his half-brother Amnon.

Absalom turned the hearts of many of the men of Israel against David and took his throne. He defiled his father's concubines and sent the men of Israel out to hunt down and kill David. The plot failed, and Absalom was killed.

Three of David's sons died because he had exposed his family to the enemies of God by his transgression.

I have seen ministers' children who are on drugs, hostile to church and bound to lust and homosexuality because their parents forfeited their positions in the spirit through transgression. We need to take the Bible seriously when it says: "Not many of you should presume to be teachers, my brothers, because you know that we who teach will be judged more strictly" (James 3:1, NIV). The reason teachers (pastors) are judged more strictly is because of the great impact of their disobedience. They not only hurt themselves but all those placed under their guardianship as well. God forgives them just as He did David. However, they will still reap what they sow. The enemy is given *place!*

I realize these are hard words. I appeal to you with all humility and write these words with fear and trembling. We have seen too many tragedies, especially in ministries. We must not judge or condemn. We need to forgive and reach out to those who have failed. If they repent, they will be forgiven by God. But I write these words as instruction and warning to those the enemy will target. We all must walk in humility and restoration.

I have four sons. I have come to realize the awesome responsibility and accountability I have for their lives. They are God's, and I am just a steward placed over them. I never want to see their lives devastated because I gave place to the devil.

When I was in the ministry of serving, I took care of menial things so those I served could go about fulfilling God's call on their lives. I took care of the dry cleaning, picked up their children from school, washed their cars and so on. One day God spoke something to me that gave me a sobering outlook on the ministry. He said, "Son, if you mess up in this position, it can be easily corrected because you're dealing with natural things. But when I place you in a ministry position, you are over people and lives are at stake."

Relinquishing Authority

The purpose of this chapter was to render an understanding of spiritual position and authority. We have seen examples of several people who lost or gave up their authority to the enemy of God. Satan will blatantly try to steal your authority by bringing sin into your life. If you are determined to serve God with all your heart, he will also try to knock you out of your position in Christ through intimidation.

The first step to breaking intimidation is to confront the matters in your own heart. In the next chapter I will describe how to do that.

Revelation is of no value without the wisdom and character to live it out.

Chapter 3

TWO EXTREMES

In just a few moments the Spirit of God can drop a wealth of insight into your spirit. But that revelation is of no value without the wisdom and character to live it out.

When the Holy Spirit led me through the scriptures about confronting intimidation, He showed me two extremes that will throw a believer's life out of balance: The first extreme is pursuing power; the second is false humility. The proper balance is found in the life of Timothy, who cultivated godly character rather than false humility and stirred up his gift rather than pursue power.

A Pure Heart

It was in Lystra that the apostle Paul first met Timothy,

a young man whose mother was a Christian Jew and whose father was Greek.

Paul wanted Timothy to accompany him and Silas as their traveling assistant. He would be responsible to care for the needs of Paul (Acts 19:22).

As time went by Timothy's faithfulness as a servant was proved. He was promoted and entrusted as a minister of the gospel, eventually pastoring the church in Ephesus. In his second letter to Timothy Paul wrote:

> I call to remembrance the genuine faith that is in you, which dwelt first in your grandmother Lois and your mother Eunice, and I am persuaded is in you also. Therefore I remind you to stir up the gift of God (2 Tim. 1:5-6).

Notice Paul references the fact that Timothy's faith was genuine. This young man's heart was pure. He was not a charlatan. In another letter Paul commends, "But I trust in the Lord Jesus to send Timothy to you shortly...for I have no one like-minded, who will sincerely care for your state. For all seek their own, not the things which are of Christ Jesus. But you know his proven character, that as a son with his father he served with me in the gospel" (Phil. 2:19-22).

It is clear that Timothy's character was not in question. As Christians, character should be our first priority and pursuit. What our Father looks for is not power, but character. It is a sad fact that many in the church pursue the power and anointing of the Spirit while sidestepping the pursuit of godly character. First Corinthians 14:1 instructs us to "pursue love, and desire spiritual gifts." However, we have perverted that command. We *pursue* the gifts and the anointing and just *wish* for the fruit of love in our lives. God is love, and until we walk in love we will not attain His nature.

One Extreme: Pursuing Power
Rather Than Character

Some Christians will travel great distances — hundreds of miles — to go to a miracle, prophetic or anointing service, but they are unwilling to deal with the anger, unforgiveness or bitterness in their own hearts. This is evidence that their emphasis is on power rather than character.

The spiritual manifestations at these services may be of God, but we have to deal with the inner man too. This unwillingness to deal with the inward has opened up many to deception. Even though the church is experiencing a refreshing at this time, sin must be dealt with. It is wonderful that people are so hungry for the power of God, but let's not neglect purity of heart.

We have seen too many ministers fall. But they didn't fall when they committed their first act of immorality. No, they began to fall earlier — the day success in ministry became more important than their intimate relationship with God. We've not only seen this among ministers but also within their congregations.

Jesus said, "Blessed are the pure in heart, for they shall see God" (Matt. 5:8). He did not say, "Blessed are those who have a successful ministry." He said that without a pure heart you will not see God! Of course, Jesus is the only one who can give us a pure heart. It is not something we can earn. It is both priceless and free — priceless in that it required the death of God's Son, and free in that it is given without cost to all who will seek Him.

I used to pray, "God, use me to win the lost. Use me to heal multitudes and deliver the masses." I would pray this over and over, and that was the extent of my seeking after God. My highest goal was to be a successful minister.

Then one day Jesus showed me that my emphasis was off. He shocked me by saying, "John, Judas cast out devils, healed the sick and preached the gospel. He left his business to become My disciple, but where is he today?" This hit me like a ton of bricks! He continued, "The goal of the high call of Christianity is not the power of God or ministry; it is to know Me." (see Phil. 3:10-15).

Later, as my wife prayed to be used along these same lines, Jesus questioned her, "Lisa, have you ever been used by a friend?"

"Yes," she answered.

"How did you feel?"

She answered, "I felt betrayed!"

He went on, "Lisa, I don't use people. I anoint, heal, transform and conform them to My image, but I don't use them."

How would you describe the marriage relationship of a woman whose only ambition was to produce children for her husband? She would only be intimate when it would produce the offspring she wanted; she would have no interest in knowing her husband personally.

I know that sounds absurd, yet how different is it from our cry for God to "use us to get people saved" when we ourselves don't enjoy relationship and fellowship with Him? When we are intimate with God, we will reproduce the way He intends: "The people who know their God shall be strong, and carry out great exploits" (Dan. 11:32).

Paul's sole ambition was to know Him (Phil. 3:8-10). Moses said, "Show me now Your way, that I may know You" (Ex. 33:13). David cried, "One thing I have desired of the Lord, that will I seek: that I may dwell in the house of the Lord all the days of my life, to behold the beauty of the Lord, and to inquire in His temple" (Ps. 27:4). And again, "My soul thirsts for You; My flesh longs for You" (Ps. 63:1).

The men and women of the Bible who desired to know God more than anything else stayed faithful to Him, finishing the course He set before them. They learned the secret of integrity with power. Seeking Him earnestly, they glimpsed His very heart.

Some people gauge their spiritual maturity by their ability to prophesy or flow in the gifts. Yet remember, gifts are given, not earned. A donkey spoke and saw into the realm of the spirit. A rooster crowed three times and convicted Peter. Does that make these beasts spiritual?

Jesus said that many would call Him Lord and expect entrance into His kingdom, only to be denied. They will have done miracles, cast out devils and prophesied in His name. But He will answer, "Depart from Me, you who practice lawlessness!" (Matt. 7:23).

The anointing of God is not His approval. Saul prophesied after God had rejected him (1 Sam. 19:23-24). Caiaphas prophesied while his one goal was to kill God's Son (John 11:49-51). We must have God's heart to be able to obey His will. Without it we will walk in merely a shadow of His anointing, troubled by legalism or lasciviousness. Balaam prophesied, and his prophecies proved true; however, he died the death of a soothsayer, put to the sword when Israel invaded the promised land.

Paul measured Timothy's virtues by the purity of his heart and the faithfulness of his service. We must also set this standard before us and allow the Holy Spirit to accurately weigh us. This extremely important prerequisite cannot be overemphasized as we go into battle with the spirit of intimidation. Without this undergirding, the truth in this message will not set you free and could possibly do you more damage than good. For it is not the words themselves that carry the power to liberate, but it is the spirit and substance behind them.

To explain this we recall what Peter warned: "As also our beloved brother Paul, according to the wisdom given to him, has written to you, as also in all his epistles, speaking in them of these things, in which are some things hard to understand, which untaught and unstable people twist to their own destruction, as they do also the rest of the Scriptures" (2 Pet. 3:15-16).

It is more important that we pursue a right relationship with God than a formula to move in His power. In light of this, examine Paul's opening statements in 2 Timothy. After establishing Timothy's pureness of heart, Paul wrote: "Therefore I remind you to stir up the gift of God" (2 Tim. 1:6). The word *therefore* means "for that reason." So Paul's instructions to Timothy concerning the release of the gift of God in Timothy's life would be invalid if his faith was not genuine. Now let's continue.

The Other Extreme: False Humility

> When I call to remembrance the genuine faith that is in you, which dwelt first in your grandmother Lois and your mother Eunice, and I am persuaded is in you also. Therefore I remind you to stir up the gift of God which is in you through the laying on of my hands (2 Tim. 1:5-6).

"Therefore I remind you." Paul was referring to his first letter to Timothy in which he exhorted, "Do not neglect the gift that is in you, which was given to you by prophecy with the laying on of the hands of the eldership" (1 Tim. 4:14). Paul stressed to Timothy the importance of not neglecting the gift of God by writing about it a second time and by making it one of the first things he mentioned in the letter.

To elaborate on what it means not to neglect the gift, let's look at some antonyms. The opposite of neglect is to:

> Accomplish, achieve, act, attend, care for, complete, conclude, consider, consummate.

All of these are words of action and authority. Most words have both a verb and a noun form. They are positive and decisive. To further rightly divide the word of God let's examine what it means to neglect:

> Breach, disdain, dismiss, disregard, discount, ignore, underestimate, overlook, undervalue, scorn, despise.

These are all negative words signifying a lack of action, decisiveness and authority. It is a serious and weighty thing to neglect what is entrusted to us. We suffer loss when we neglect.

The opposite extreme of simply pursuing the power is living in what I describe as a state of false humility. People living in such a state recognize the importance of pursuing God's character but stop there. They never venture out into God's gifting in their lives because they are afraid. They avoid anything that involves confrontation, perceiving it as a lack of love or Christian character.

I refer to these people as "peacekeepers." At first glance peacekeeping may look appealing, but Jesus never said, "Blessed are the peacekeepers." Rather, He said, "Blessed are the peacemakers, for they shall be called sons of God" (Matt. 5:9). A peacekeeper avoids confrontation at any cost. He will go to any length to preserve a false sense of security for himself, which he mistakes for peace.

A peacemaker, on the other hand, will boldly confront no matter what it may cost him because he does not worry about himself. Instead, he is motivated by his love for God and truth. Only under these conditions can true peace thrive.

There is peace in the kingdom of God (Rom. 14:17). However, this peace does not come by the absence of confrontation. As Jesus pointed out, "The kingdom of heaven suffers violence, and the violent take it by force"

(Matt. 11:12). There is violent opposition to the advancement of God's kingdom.

Often we think, I'll just ignore this, and it will go away. But we need to wake up and realize that what we do not confront will not change! This is why Jude urges on the saints with the following:

> Beloved, while I was very diligent to write to you concerning our common salvation, I found it necessary to write to you exhorting you to contend earnestly for the faith which was once for all delivered to the saints (Jude 3).

Notice he said "contend earnestly," not hope for the best. Contend means to fight or wage battle. Christianity is not an easy lifestyle! There is constant opposition and resistance to our pursuit of God in both the natural and the spiritual realms!

Paul strengthened Timothy with, "You therefore must endure hardship as a good soldier of Jesus Christ. No one engaged in warfare entangles himself..." (2 Tim. 2:3-4). We are engaged in warfare. We are to have the attitude of a soldier. We are not to back down from evil, but we are to overcome it with good by God's grace (Rom. 12:21).

The letters from Paul were Timothy's marching orders as he pastored at Ephesus. Timothy faced challenges. There was false doctrine to be exposed, strife and contention to be stopped and leaders to be raised up so that a strong and mature church could develop. And these were just a few of the more obvious responsibilities he must have faced.

I'm sure there were many opportunities for confrontation. I'm sure accusation and slander were hurled against him by those within the church who were immature or wicked. Besides all this, he had another obstacle to overcome — his age. He was a young man in a church where

40

many were older. This by itself could open a door to intimidation. But in the face of all this, Paul instructed Timothy to remain strong, not forgetting what had been imparted to him. Paul constantly reminded Timothy to stand in his God-given authority. Perhaps Timothy had backed down at one time, so Paul instructed:

These things command and teach (1 Tim. 4:11).

And these things command, that they may be blameless (1 Tim. 5:7).

You therefore, my son, be strong in the grace that is in Christ Jesus (2 Tim. 2:1).

Maybe Timothy was like so many others today who love God but avoid confrontation. Fear of confrontation makes you easy prey for intimidation.

If you identify with this fear, then this message is sent to bring you courage and liberty. God wants you liberated to do and be whatever He asks of you. When you are intimidated, there is no joy. And without joy there is no strength. Where there is fear, there is no peace. But as you break out of what has held you back, you'll find joy and peace in abundance!

How does this apply to me?

Chapter 4

IMPARTED GIFTS

Up to this point we have only dealt with intimidation and its effect on leadership in the church. But it's quite possible many of you reading this book are not in full time ministry. You may be asking, How does this apply to me?

God gives a place, or position, in the spirit to each believer. Remember, Paul explained that God has "raised us up together, and made us sit together in the heavenly places in Christ Jesus" (Eph. 2:6). This is where the redeemed children of God are to dwell. Its location is "far above all principality and power and might and dominion, and every name that is named, not only in this age but also in that which is to come. And He put all things under His feet, and gave Him [the Lord Jesus] to be head over all things to the church, which is His body" (Eph. 1:21-23).

The church is the body of Christ. Just as our physical bodies contain many parts that differ in function and ability, even so the members of the body of Christ function in different callings and gifts. God determines their purpose and function. Each is important, and none is independent from the others.

Paul declared that all demonic spirits were placed under the feet of Jesus. This clearly illustrates that no devil should exercise authority over a believer. If you are the foot of the body of Christ, the demons are still under you. Jesus said, "Behold, I give you the authority ...over all the power of the enemy, and nothing shall by any means hurt you" (Luke 10:19). However, if we don't exercise or walk in our God-given authority, someone will take it from us and use it against us! The enemy is after our position in the spirit.

Gifted to Function

Let's continue in our study of Paul's letter to Timothy.

> Therefore I remind you to stir up the gift of God which is in you through the laying on of my hands (2 Tim. 1:6).

The Greek word for gift is *charisma*. Strong's concordance defines the word as "a spiritual endowment." Another definition, adapted from Vine's dictionary, would be "a gift of grace endowed upon believers by the operation of the Holy Spirit." So the word *charisma* describes those spiritual abilities with which God equips believers.

Nothing in the realm of the spirit is accomplished without this *charisma,* or supernatural ability of God.

We should not preach, sing, prophesy, lead or even serve without it. There is no life produced without this grace. Lifeless religion is born out of man's attempt to serve God his own way, in his own ability. When we minister to others without the gifting of God, we labor in vain.

Notice that this gift was already resident inside Timothy. When the Lord plants His gift, it does not come and go but abides within. "For the gifts [*charisma*] and the calling of God are irrevocable" (Rom. 11:29). This gift, or power, is the equipment necessary to fulfill the call God places on each of us. Functioning in these gifts should be natural and comfortable for us. Just as the roles and functions of our individual parts don't vary or come and go, so it is with the gifts God imparts.

Paul wrote to the Roman believers, "I long to see you, that I may impart to you some spiritual gift [*charisma*], so that you may be established" (Rom. 1:11). The church will not be established without these gifts, the spiritual equipment that enables God's children to bring forth His will. Carefully read the following verse:

> As each one has received a gift [*charisma*], minister it to one another, as good stewards of the manifold grace of God (1 Pet. 4:10).

We will examine three issues in this verse:

1. Everyone receives a gift.

2. The gift is not ours; we are merely stewards of it.

3. The gift is a portion of God's manifold grace.

1. Everyone receives a gift.

Notice it says, "As each one has received a gift, minister it." Peter did not say, "As the select few have received gifts." No, if you are born again and Spirit-filled, you have received God's gift to function in His body. There are no lame, useless parts in this body.

Paul says in Ephesians 4:7, "But to each one of us grace was given according to the measure of Christ's gift." And again in 1 Corinthians 7:7, "For I wish that all men were even as I myself. But each one has his own gift from God, one in this manner and another in that."

If we are ignorant of this we remain unable or unfit for service. Thus, our call goes unfulfilled. Just as babies learn to use their body parts, we must develop and exercise this gifting for service in His body. No part of His body operates outside of this supernatural ability.

2. The gift is not ours; we are merely stewards of it.

Since we do not own it, this gift is not to be neglected or used for personal gain. It is not ours to do with as we please. It is given that we might serve others. We are accountable for our care of it.

Recall the parable of the talents. The master delivered "to one...five talents, to another two, and to another one, to each according to his own ability" (Matt. 25:15). He then went away on a journey. The first two men used their talents wisely, bringing increase, while the third man buried his.

When the master returned, the first two gave an account of what was done with the talents entrusted to them. The master commended each of them, "Well done, good and faithful servant."

Then the third man came to give account. In fear he

had hidden his talent. He perceived his master as unfair, as one who expected too much. So this servant felt justified in his neglect, selfishness and carelessness. Essentially, he told his master, "Look, you have what is yours."

When the master saw how this servant despised what was committed to his care, he called him wicked and lazy. His one talent was taken away and given to the man who had doubled his. Then the unprofitable servant was cast out (Matt. 25:16-30).

We will give an account for the gifts entrusted to us, as all stewards give account of their stewardship. Another word for gift is *ability,* which is defined as "capability, faculty, genius or power." In other words, talent. From this parable we see a vivid illustration of the importance of nurturing and developing the gift, ability or talent God has trusted us with.

Paul was entrusted with a ministry of teaching and apostleship. He said, "I became a minister according to the gift of the grace of God given to me by the effective working of His power" (Eph. 3:7). Notice the importance he placed on being faithful to the gift:

> For if I preach the gospel, I have nothing to boast of, for necessity is laid upon me; yes, woe is me if I do not preach the gospel! For if I do this willingly, I have a reward; but if against my will, I have been entrusted with a stewardship (1 Cor. 9:16-17).

Paul says, "Woe is me." Now *woe* is a very strong word. Jesus used it to warn of the pending judgment of certain individuals or cities. He said woe to Chorazin and Bethsaida, cities that no longer exist (Matt. 11:21-22). He said woe to the scribes and Pharisees (Matt. 23), and to Judas (Matt. 26:24).

Woe is used by Jude to describe the judgment of evil

men in the church. In the book of Revelation it is used in reference to the inhabitants of the earth under God's judgment (Rev. 8:13). By using the word *woe,* Paul indicated the awesome responsibility of faithfulness to God's gift.

A Christian will backslide when he does not function in his gift or calling, just as a muscle atrophies with lack of use. An idle believer isolates himself, becoming easy prey for the enemy.

While studying the lives of great men and women of God, I found that those who fell had become idle or negligent in their call. Perhaps they were still ministering, but it was under the natural momentum achieved by their previous years of ministry. They began to use God's gift for their own benefit, not to protect and serve others.

King David fell into sin when he should have been at battle.

> It happened in the spring of the year, at the time when kings go out to battle, that David sent Joab and his servants with him, and all Israel; and they destroyed the people of Ammon and besieged Rabbah. But David remained at Jerusalem (2 Sam. 11:1).

David was king. God made him a king to shepherd and protect Israel. It was time for him to battle, not to stay home in Jerusalem enjoying the rewards of past victories. He was relaxing, riding on the benefits of his earlier labors. Bored, he scanned his domain from the balcony and saw Bathsheba bathing. The rest is history.

The point is, we are not here to take a vacation. Our lives are not even our own, for even they were purchased and given back to us for stewardship. We're sojourners, not permanent residents. Too many people act as if this life were their final destination!

Jesus said, "My food is to do the will of Him who sent Me, and to finish His work" (John 4:34). This should be our diet also. Jesus knew what was necessary to maintain His strength. Our strength is drawn from food, both physical and spiritual. If we cease to do His will, using His provisions for our own benefit, we become weary and lose strength, just as we would if we had stopped eating. With this loss of strength we find it easier to flow with this world, not against it. We become self-willed, self-centered, self-conscious and self-serving.

We have a great responsibility. We should not be people who go to church, apply nothing to our lives and become fat off the Word of God. God warns in Ezekiel 34:20, "Therefore thus says the Lord God to them: 'Behold, I Myself will judge between the fat and the lean sheep.'"

Who are the fat sheep? The ones who serve themselves with the good things of God to the neglect of others. Watch how God describes the fat sheep.

> Is it too little for you to have eaten up the good pasture, that you must tread down with your feet the residue of your pasture — and to have drunk of the clear waters, that you must foul the residue with your feet?
>
> You have pushed with side and shoulder, butted all the weak ones with your horns, and scattered them abroad, therefore I will save My flock, and they shall no longer be a prey; and I will judge between sheep and sheep (Ezek. 34:18,21-22).

God's gifts are not for our excess. God will test us with His goodness. We are to use the ability of God in our life to serve those who are weak, young or unable so that the body might be whole.

Don't misunderstand. It is right for us to enjoy the fruit of our labor. God gives us both rest and refreshing. But when our focus revolves around only ourselves, we become fat and careless. Gifts and talents used only to serve ourselves are not multiplied.

Each part of your body is accountable to the other parts. If your legs refused to work, your whole body would suffer. If your lungs or heart decided to stop, your other members would perish! If Satan can get us to focus on ourselves instead of serving others, then the entire body will suffer.

3. The gift is a portion of God's manifold grace.

The key word is *manifold* or "many fold." Peter divides gifts into two major categories. The first is the oracle or speaking gift; the second, the ministry or serving gift. "If anyone speaks, let him speak as the oracles of God. If anyone ministers, let him do it as with the ability which God supplies" (1 Pet. 4:11).

Paul further divides these two categories. Look at this passage from the book of Romans.

> For as we have many members in one body, but all the members do not have the same function, so we, being many, are one body in Christ, and individually members of one another.
>
> Having then gifts differing according to the grace that is given to us, let us use them: if prophecy, let us prophesy in proportion to our faith; or ministry, let us use it in our ministering; he who teaches, in teaching; he who exhorts, in exhortation; he who gives, with liberality; he who leads, with diligence; he who shows mercy, with cheerfulness (Rom. 12:4-8).

Under the oracle category we find prophecy, teaching, exhortation and leading; under the serving category are ministry (serving), giving and mercy.

Let me interject this point. You should not be in an oracle, or leader, position until you have proved faithful in serving one who is. There are many who want to lead and preach who have not laid their lives down to serve. No matter how talented they are, it is a disservice to both them and those under their care. If their character is not developed through serving, they will use their leadership position to lord it over people.

I have seen two extremes resulting from a lack of understanding. The first deals with those who think more highly of themselves than they ought. Mistaking the oracle for the only gift, they think it is the pinnacle of ministry and don't believe there is any other way to serve God.

This is incorrect. "For in fact the body is not one member but many...If the whole body were an eye, where would be the hearing? If the whole were hearing, where would be the smelling?" (1 Cor. 12:14,17). They all want to be a mouth. Every part is important. Without the ministry of helps, the oracle ministry is limited. People try to move in a gift they *want* rather than the one they *have!*

The other extreme is those who believe ministry is limited to preachers or ministry staff. This mentality cripples the body, causing it to function at the level of an invalid.

Paul explains, "No, much rather, those members of the body which seem to be weaker are necessary. And those members of the body which we think to be less honorable, on these we bestow greater honor" (1 Cor. 12:22-23). This elevates the importance of the unnoticed. God made the unseen even more crucial than the seen. You can live without a voice but not without a liver or heart. Without these there would be no walking or talking.

The book of Acts shows the attitude toward gifts in the early church. The early Christians realized there was much more to ministry than preaching, healing, deliverance and prophesying. Acts 6 mentions that some widows in the church of Jerusalem were neglected. They needed meals and help with other daily needs.

When this came to the attention of the leadership, they responded, "Therefore, brethren, seek out from among you seven men of good reputation, full of the Holy Spirit and wisdom, whom we may appoint over this business" (Acts 6:3). They found men who met these qualifications and brought them before the apostles. "When they had prayed, they laid hands on them. Then the word of God spread, and the number of the disciples multiplied greatly in Jerusalem" (Acts 6:6-7).

What happened when they laid hands on them? The gift to serve was imparted, and as a result, the word of God spread and disciples multiplied. These men operated in the gift that was given to them. What an amazing fact. Men serving widows caused the word of God to spread and the disciples to greatly multiply!

I believe one of the big reasons our churches are not growing and multiplying is because not all the people (congregations *and* leaders) are moving in their gifts. The book of Acts even demonstrates how a leader who is operating in the gifts can bring a limited number of people to salvation, but when the whole church gets involved, the results are much greater.

Right after the day of Pentecost, when Peter preached, "that day about three thousand souls were *added* to them" (Acts 2:41, italics added; see also v. 47). Even when Peter walked the streets of Jerusalem under a healing anointing, "believers were increasingly *added* to the Lord, multitudes of both men and women" (Acts 5:14).

But when believers began to teach every day in every house (Acts 5:42), then the church began "multiplying" (Acts 6:1). The next step was for believers to serve, which was begun with the ministry to widows. After that point, the church "multiplied greatly" (Acts 6:7).

Today pastors practically beg for volunteers. How sad. You don't see the leaders in the book of Acts asking for volunteers. They took these serving positions so seriously that they searched out qualified men to wait tables — qualified on the basis of character, not talent. Then they were appointed. What importance they placed on something that today we consider trivial.

Responsibility to Be Faithful

What would happen if all believers functioned in their place? What tremendous things we would see. Revival is not for the preachers but for the entire body — when every person takes his position.

Remember, the gift is the ability God gives us. We are not responsible for that which we were not entrusted with. The leg is not responsible for sight. Even so, the will of God can only be accomplished by the enabling of the Spirit. "Not that we are sufficient of ourselves to think of anything as being from ourselves, but our sufficiency is from God" (2 Cor. 3:5).

It is the joint operation of these gifts the enemy wants to stop. When successful he can severely hinder our growth! He knows he cannot stop God from giving these gifts, so he is after our freedom to exercise them. Intimidation is the primary way he hinders this.

EXPOSING
INTIMIDATION

Why are so many of us ineffective?

Chapter 5

DORMANT GIFTS

We have established that every believer holds a position of authority that comes with God-given talents or gifts and is hidden in Christ Jesus above all demonic authority. So why are so many of us ineffective? To answer that, let's again read Paul's reminder to Timothy:

> Therefore I remind you to stir up the gift of God which is in you through the laying on of my hands (2 Tim. 1:6).

The Greek word for "stir up" is *anazopureo*, which means "to kindle afresh or keep in full flame" (Vine's dictionary). If Paul had to encourage this young man to stir up or kindle the gift (*charisma*), then it can become dormant! The gift does not work automatically. Like a fire it must be stirred up and kept going!

There are those with pure hearts and true intentions who believe that if God wants something to happen, it will just happen. But this is incorrect. Edmund Burke wrote in 1795: "The only thing necessary for the triumph of evil is for good men to do nothing "[1]

Timothy was pure in heart. Remember how Paul extolled his character? "For I have no one like-minded, who will sincerely care for your state. For all seek their own, not the things which are of Christ Jesus. But you know his proven character" (Phil. 2:19-22). Yet it is Paul who warned him twice not to neglect the gift of God, causing it to remain dormant.

So there are two questions we need to answer: What causes the gift to become dormant? How do we stir it up? I will answer the second question in a later chapter, but let's look at the first one now. What causes the gift of God to lie dormant?

The answer is in the following verse:

> Therefore I remind you to stir up the gift of God which is in you through the laying on of my hands. For [because] God has not given us a spirit of fear, but of power and of love and of a sound mind (2 Tim. 1:6-7).

The Greek word for fear is *deilia*. The word implies timidity and cowardice, and is never used in a good sense in Scripture (Vine's dictionary). Looking again at verse 7 from the New International Version:

> For God did not give us a spirit of timidity (2 Tim. 1:7).

The translators of the NIV believe *timidity* is the most accurate word for this verse, and so do I. In this light, Paul is telling Timothy, "Your gift of God is dormant because of timidity." Without changing the meaning, I could say:

> Timothy, the gift of God in you lies dormant because of intimidation!

Intimidated believers lose their authority in the spirit by default; consequently, their gift — God's ability in them — lies asleep and inactive. Though it is present, it is not in operation.

When that elder in Michigan told me the praise and worship leaders thought I was being too hard on them, I was intimidated. Suddenly the gift of God was inactive, and I didn't preach under the anointing as I had in the previous eighteen services. The life of God appeared to be gone. Confusion set in; I lost my decisiveness; I didn't want to face the people. Why? Because I was intimidated, and therefore I yielded my God-given authority.

Intimidation Defined

Now let's look at the definitions of *intimidate* and *intimidation*. The *Oxford English Dictionary* defines *intimidate* as:

1. to render timid.
2. to inspire with fear.
3. to overawe, cow.[2]

Merriam-Webster's Collegiate Dictionary (Tenth ed.) defines *intimidate* as:

> to discourage, coerce, or suppress by (or as if by) threatening.[3]

The *Oxford English Dictionary* defines *intimidation* as:

1. the action of intimidating or making afraid.

2. the fact or condition of being intimidated.

3. the use of threats or violence to force or restrain from some action.[4]

The objective of intimidation is to restrain you from action, and coerce or force you into submission. Intimidation wants to overwhelm you with a sense of inferiority and fear. Once you've retreated into submission, either knowingly or unknowingly, you are a servant of the intimidator. You are no longer free to fulfill the will of God but are doomed to the desires of your intimidating captor.

Consequently, the gift of God, His spiritual ability in you, is inoperative. Now your authority has been stripped from you in order to be used against both you and those in your sphere of influence.

The origin of intimidation is fear, which has its root in our adversary, the devil. He is the originator of all fear and timidity (Gen. 3:1-10, especially v. 10). He will attack us by way of thoughts, imaginations and visions, or he will use circumstances and those under his influence to intimidate us. Either way, he has one objective: to control and limit us.

Elijah Intimidated?

Elijah the prophet operated in tremendous power. He stood boldly before a wicked king who had no fear of God and declared, "There shall not be dew nor rain these years, except at my word" (1 Kin. 17:1). He was not afraid of this godless king.

He spent the next few years living in the miraculous. First he was fed by ravens; then he was sustained by a widow whose meal and oil would not run out though famine and starvation were all around them. This widow's son suddenly died, and God heard the prayer of Elijah, raising the boy from the dead. This was a man with a powerful ministry.

After a long period of time he again stood before the king. The king blamed Elijah for the hardship and suffering from the drought and greeted him with, "Is that you, O troubler of Israel?" (1 Kin. 18:17).

Elijah boldly answered, "I have not troubled Israel, but you and your father's house have, in that you have forsaken the commandments of the Lord and followed the Baals" (1 Kin. 18:18). Then he commanded the king to gather up the 850 prophets of Baal and Asherah and take them to Mt. Carmel — along with the entire nation of Israel.

On the day of the confrontation all of Israel assembled to see who was the true God! Elijah boldly challenged the prophets of Baal and Asherah to offer a sacrifice to their gods at the same time he offered one to the Lord. "And the God who answers by fire, He is God," Elijah declared (1 Kin. 18:24).

The Lord God answered by fire, and the people of Israel fell on their faces and turned back to God. Then, under the orders of Elijah, they killed all 850 false prophets.

Next, Elijah proclaimed it would rain, earnestly praying and calling it forth when there was no sign of rain. In minutes the sky became black, and a heavy rain fell. As Ahab fled to his palace the hand of God came upon Elijah, and he outran Ahab's chariot.

This was just one day in the life of Elijah. The nation turned around; the wicked were slain; the long drought was over. Elijah could clearly hear the voice of God, act on it and see great miracles.

Confronted by the King's Wife

But on the very same day Ahab's wife, Jezebel, heard

what was done to her prophets and sent a message to Elijah: "So let the gods do to me, and more also, if I do not make your life as the life of one of them by tomorrow about this time" (1 Kin. 19:2). She was enraged with him, for those were her prophets, preaching her message. Now look at Elijah's response:

> And when he saw that, he arose and ran for his life, and went to Beersheba, which belongs to Judah, and left his servant there. But he himself went a day's journey into the wilderness, and came and sat down under a broom tree. And he prayed that he might die, and said, "It is enough! Now, Lord, take my life, for I am no better than my fathers!" (1 Kin. 19:3-4).

The same day he won so great a battle, he ran for his life. He was so intimidated and discouraged by Jezebel that he wanted to die. The purpose of her intimidation was to prevent Elijah from completing God's purpose. She wanted to reverse his influence over the nation. She wanted him destroyed and out of the way. Even though she couldn't kill him, she still accomplished one goal by terrifying him into running away and wishing for death. Unwittingly, he was cooperating with her plan. If he could have seen clearer he would have never run.

Symptoms of Intimidation

An intimidating spirit unleashes confusion, discouragement and frustration. Its goal is to cause you to lose your proper perspective. Everything will seem overwhelming, difficult or even impossible. The stronger the intimidation, the greater the discouragement and hopelessness. If intimidation is not dealt with immediately, it will cause you to do things you never would do if you were not

SU-JUBES

Yum! Yum!

Heather Lauren

Old Dutch POTATO CHIPS

← T-shirt

The Voyage of the Dawn Treader

Blue Returns

Blue Punch buggy

Liz

Jill Shopkins

200

Phoebe

Rachel

Sophie

KID'S TRAVEL BACKSEAT SURVIVAL KIT

Bug Safe!

Holidays

I fell good, I knew that I would

Book Light   JUICY FRUIT

ODYSSEES TAPES

← Shorts

LAURA'S ACTIVITY BOOK

PARTY MIX

AMBER

"Yellow ear..." jelly bean!

- We need to be World changers.
- 95% never shared christ
- Is. 55 1-3
- Why spend energy on things do not satysfy
- Have Fun!
- You can watch T.V., Computer
- Read the Bible — not the T.V. guide
- 2 kings 4:1-7
- Have a higher RQ - how much of Gods spirit you recieve from him
- How badly do you want God?

- Prayer changes things.
- Be presistant in prayer.
- Devote time to prayer
- Stay on your knees
- pictures
- visions
- grief of holy spirit
- God wants to bring conviction of sin

Incredible Love of God for his bride

- God longs for his peoples heart
- He wants our hearts
- Luke 15 - The Lost Son
- The church is not well feed spiritualy.
- 9% speaks english 90% different
  missions reach these people
- Us - 1 million
  - Then - 3 thousand
- pray for missionaries
- Richest church (American)

under its influence. This is exactly the goal of intimidation.

Examining instances when I've been attacked by an intimidating spirit, I can relate to what Elijah must have felt. Before I understood how intimidation worked, I would sit in my hotel room fighting discouragement and hopelessness. I would wonder, What good is all this doing? Who do you think you are? I would sometimes even have these thoughts in the morning after a great service.

I recall one particular time when I could do absolutely nothing all day. I couldn't shake the heaviness. I would pray, and it seemed God was nowhere. Just as with Elijah, my focus had shifted to me, me, me. I felt ineffective; I considered my ministry to be worthless. That is why Elijah said, "It is enough! Now, Lord, take my life, for I am no better than my fathers!" (1 Kin. 19:4).

At the end of this particularly discouraging day, God showed me how Elijah was intimidated by Jezebel. I finally recognized that my behavior was exactly what this intimidating, discouraging spirit wanted. It wanted me to back off from what God sent me to do. There were people in that church who did not like the message of repentance and holiness God had me bring.

I immediately went after the root of the symptoms I had struggled with all day — a spirit of intimidation. I boldly broke free and felt released from confusion and frustration. We had a powerful meeting that night! I will explain later how to confront the spirit of intimidation. But now let's look again at the life of Elijah to see how to recognize it.

What Are You Doing Here?

Elijah was knocked out of his authority when he did not confront Jezebel's intimidation head on. As a result, his ministry gift to the nation was suppressed, and he went in a direction that was not God's desire. I'm sure he looked like quite a different man as he ran *away* from the confrontation he earlier ran *into*. He headed in the opposite direction, dropping off his servant and running forty days and nights to Mount Horeb. The first thing he heard God say upon arriving was, "What are you doing here, Elijah?" (1 Kin. 19:9).

Can you imagine? He is discouraged to the point of death, exhausted from running for forty days and in a state of depression. And God asks, "Why are you here?" Was God saying, "Why did you run from your post and hide here?"

You may be thinking, Well, God sent the angel who gave Elijah the two cakes so he could run for forty days and nights. Why would God ask, "What are you doing here?"

God knew Elijah was determined to run. When a man has it in his heart to do something, God will often let him do it even if it is not His perfect will.

God did the same thing with Balaam when he was asked by Balak, king of Moab, to come and curse Israel. The Lord told Balaam not to go. But Balaam went back and asked God a second time, and it appeared God had a change of heart. He told Balaam to go.

The next morning Balaam saddled his donkey to go, and the Bible says, "Then God's anger was aroused because he went" (Num. 22:22). An angel of God came to kill him.

Why did God tell him to go and then become angry when he did? God let Balaam go because He knew his heart. He knew Balaam wanted the honor and money Balak was offering more than he wanted to obey God. When a man sets his heart to do something, God will not stop him, even if it is not God's perfect will.

This was the case with Elijah. God desired him to go back and confront Jezebel as he had the prophets of Baal. That would complete what was begun on Mount Carmel.

But Elijah did not want to face her. He wanted out of the pressure he was under. So God sent an angel to him to give him the necessary food for his journey. God would wait and deal with Elijah's intimidation once he reached Mount Horeb.

The One Behind It All

The work God had begun through Elijah could not be completed until Jezebel was confronted. She was at the very root of Israel's problem. The Bible says, "But there was no one like Ahab who sold himself to do wickedness in the sight of the Lord, because Jezebel his wife stirred him up" (1 Kin. 21:25). The Lord would have been with Elijah had he not fled, just as He had been with him on Mount Carmel. But he was intimidated by Jezebel and was knocked out of his authority. The gift to finish the task was dormant.

Now look at what God says to Elijah after asking twice why he was there.

> Then the Lord said to him: "Go, return on your way to the Wilderness of Damascus; and when you arrive, anoint Hazael as king over Syria. Also you shall anoint Jehu the son of Nimshi as king over Israel. And Elisha the son of Shaphat of Abel Meholah you shall anoint as prophet in your place. It shall be that whoever escapes the sword of Hazael, Jehu will kill; and whoever escapes the sword of Jehu, Elisha will kill" (1 Kin. 19:15-17).

Notice He told Elijah to anoint Elisha as prophet in his *place* and to anoint Jehu as king over Israel. God had two other men who would not run from Jezebel. They would complete his assignment.

The work Elijah had begun was put on hold as he ran from Jezebel's intimidation. Remember, Jezebel was the motivating influence behind the wickedness that had crept into Israel. If the wrong influence of a leader is not confronted and put to a stop, then it is only a matter of time before the wickedness filters down to those under their charge.

Jesus taught this principle, "No one can enter a strong man's house and plunder his goods, unless he first binds the strong man. And then he will plunder his house" (Mark 3:27). The strong man is the leader; the house is his domain or territory of influence; his goods, the fruit or result of his influence. Now applying these interpretations read again what Jesus said:

> No one can enter a leader's territory and plunder the results of his influence unless he first puts a stop to the leader. And then he will plunder his territory (Mark 3:27, author's paraphrase).

You say, But Ahab was the leader, and Elijah was not afraid of him. Yes and no. Ahab bore the title of leader, but he had yielded his authority to his wife. Therefore, in the realm of the spirit she was the "strong man" over the idolatry in Israel. She was the instigator of the Baal worship. It was her influence that caused the entire nation of Israel, with the exception of the seven thousand faithful to God, to depart from the worship of the one true God. Since she was not directly confronted, her influence remained.

I have seen this time and time again. There are those who bear the title of pastor or leader, yet they are controlled by the manipulation and intimidation of others — usually the people who should be undergirding them, such as wives, associates, board members, deacons, intercessors and so forth. They run the show behind the scenes by controlling the person with the title of leader.

This also happens in homes. Parents are intimidated by their children; husbands are intimidated by their wives. They are not the head of their homes. It is important for a leader to consider the counsel of those around him, whether in his home or his ministry. But it is more important that he stays in his authority so he can serve and protect his family or ministry using the gift God has given him.

If you continue to read the account of what happened after Elijah ran for his life, you will find that the work Elijah began had withered away. Ahab continued to oppress the people with his wickedness. Jezebel's influence over her husband — and the kingdom — grew. Baal worship was restored, even though Elijah confronted the prophets of Baal and the entire nation witnessed the power of God. When he ran from Jezebel, Elijah took with him the courage of the people of Israel. Ahab died, but his two sons who reigned after him continued to lead the nation astray and deeper into idolatry (1 Kin. 22:51–2 Kin. 9).

Two Men Who Would Not Give Up Their Authority

Elijah ran from the source of all this perversion and corruption. For this reason the Lord instructed him to anoint two men to deal with this evil woman. It was Jehu who eventually killed Jezebel (2 Kin. 9:30-37). When she tried to control him, he refused to come under her intimidation. Once confronted and destroyed, her sphere of influence fell as well (2 Kin. 10).

Jehu and his men then killed all seventy of Ahab's sons. He called all the Baal worshippers together and put them to the edge of the sword. He went into the temple of Baal and burned the sacred articles. His men broke down the pillar of Baal and tore down the temple, making it a refuse dump. Now look at what the Bible says about Jehu:

Thus Jehu destroyed Baal from Israel (2 Kin. 10:28).

God said plainly to Elijah, "Whoever escapes the sword of Jehu, Elisha will kill" (1 Kin. 19:17). It took two of them now to complete what Elijah was originally sent to do. When God told Elijah to anoint Elisha "prophet in your place," it was because Elijah had surrendered his place of authority because of intimidation. Jehu and Elisha, however, did not yield their God-given authority to any of Ahab's house; therefore, the gifting of God was not dormant, and the nation was delivered from Baal worship.

When we are intimidated, we give up our position of authority. Consequently, the gift of God to serve and protect lies dormant. We end up unintentionally furthering the cause of the one intimidating us.

There are many Old Testament accounts of God's people backing down when they should have pressed forward. As Paul wrote, "Now all these things happened to them as examples, and they were written for our admonition, upon whom the ends of the ages have come" (1 Cor. 10:11). And again to the Romans, "For whatever things were written before were written for our learning" (Rom. 15:4). I will give many Old and New Testament accounts given in this book, for we cannot fully understand the New Testament applications without the Old Testament examples. In the next chapter we'll see how intimidation hinders the work of God, not only in a leader but also in the people he serves.

An intimidated person honors what he fears more than God.

Chapter 6

PARALYZED
BY INTIMIDATION

Intimidation paralyzes us in the realm of the spirit. It causes us to compromise what we know to be right. It causes us to allow or tolerate what we, under other circumstances, wouldn't stand for.

An example of this is found in the story of Eli and his sons. Before Israel became a monarchy, it was governed by judges whom God raised up at critical times in the nation's history. According to Dake's Bible, Eli was the fifteenth judge of Israel. Not only was he judge, he also was the seventh high priest. He judged Israel for forty years. His two sons, Hophni and Phinehas, were priests as well. Now let's look at Israel's spiritual atmosphere under the leadership of Eli:

71

> And the word of the Lord was rare in those days;
> there was no widespread revelation (1 Sam. 3:1).

The word of the Lord referred to here is not the written Scriptures, for the Israelites had the Torah. This verse refers instead to the God-inspired insight into the ways and plans of God. There remained only a distant memory of God speaking openly with His people. The author of the book was now silent. His voice was rarely heard.

So why was God so quiet? We find our answer in chapter 2:

> Now Eli was very old; and he heard everything his sons did to all Israel, and how they lay with the women who assembled at the door of the tabernacle of meeting (1 Sam. 2:22).

Hophni and Phinehas, Eli's sons, were wicked. Not only were they fornicating with the women of Israel, they were so bold as to fornicate with the women who came to serve in the tabernacle, where the presence of God was to dwell. Where was their fear of God?

Their wickedness was not confined to sexual contempt. They also took by force the raw meat offerings brought by the people. This practice was contrary to the law, and it robbed the worshippers and the Lord of the meat that belonged to them. This caused the people of Israel to despise the offering of the Lord. Hophni and Phinehas were stumbling blocks to the people of Israel. Their behavior caused the people to resent the things of God.

Eli knew what his sons were doing; however, he did not remove them and only corrected them with a weak rebuke: "Why do you do such things? For I hear of your evil dealings from all the people. No, my sons! For it is not a good report that I hear. You make the Lord's people transgress" (1 Sam. 2:23-24). His sons deserved more than this light correction. They should have been removed from their position as priests and from the tabernacle altogether, since they had no heart of repentance.

A prophet of God came to Eli and said, "Why do you kick at My sacrifice and My offering which I have commanded in My dwelling place, and honor your sons more than Me?...for those who honor Me I will honor, and those who despise Me shall be lightly esteemed" (1 Sam. 2:29-30).

To honor means "to regard, esteem or respect." When Eli refused to confront and discipline his sons, he showed that he esteemed them more than God. An intimidated person honors what he fears more than he honors God. With or without realizing it, he submits to what intimidates him. If Eli hadn't been intimidated, he would have dealt with his sons differently.

Later God speaks to Samuel concerning Eli, "For I have told him that I will judge his house forever for the iniquity which he knows, because his sons made themselves vile, and he did not restrain them" (1 Sam. 3:13).

The word of the Lord was rare, and wickedness reigned unrestrained because the judge and high priest was afraid of his sons! He had lost his place of authority, and his ability to judge righteously and minister to Israel was gone. The purpose of God was thwarted. Israel's enemies grew strong on all sides while corruption reigned within. When leaders relinquish their authority, all those under their care suffer.

Does This Sound Familiar?

It is unfortunate, but many fathers are intimidated by their own children. As a youth pastor I listened to Christian families desperate for help. I saw teenagers who despised their parents. They spoke to their parents with little or absolutely no respect. It appeared their parents irritated them. Stunned, I would correct these young people right in front of their own parents because their parents were embarrassed and afraid to correct them. Their homes were chaotic; anarchy reigned. The parents had relinquished their authority to their children. The gifting or power of God in the parents to establish order in their home and raise up godly children was dormant.

This problem is not limited to our homes but is evident in our churches as well. I have been in hundreds of churches. I am alarmed to see how many leaders are intimidated by their own people. The atmosphere in their churches is not unlike that of Israel under Eli: God's voice is rare.

These leaders have given up their position of authority, and the power of God is dormant. The pastors preach at every service, and there is praise and worship, but little or no evidence of the presence of God.

The minister either carefully prepares his message so he doesn't offend or confront those in disobedience, or else he rants and raves in frustration, beating the sheep to cover up his intimidation by the few. But in all of this there is little or no spiritual life.

Rare is the biblical description of God's presence. There may be a spurt of life here or there, but God's presence does not abide, and His word is not free to flow as a fountain of living water.

The Church of the Living Dead

In 1990 I ministered at a "full gospel" church. The people thought they were alive and moving with God. As I preached Sunday morning, I felt as if my words were being hurled back in my face. It was like preaching face-to-face with a brick wall. The atmosphere was thick with rebellion.

I couldn't figure it out. The pastor and his wife were two of the sweetest people I'd ever met. Their son led praise and worship and was precious. I was baffled until

I went to lunch with them after the service.

The pastor said, "John, I have a question for you. There is a couple in my church who got divorced. They both continued to come, sitting on opposite sides of the church. Then the man, who is my head usher, met a younger woman in my church and began to date her. After a while she moved in with him. Now they're living together. What do I do?"

I couldn't believe he even needed to ask me this. Stunned, I asked, "Do you mean you haven't removed him from the church?"

"No," he answered, "but I have asked him to step down from being head usher."

I proceeded to preach to the pastor and his wife for an hour. I told them how Paul dealt with the elders at the Corinthian church. A man was living in immorality there as well. Paul rebuked them: "And you are puffed up, and have not rather mourned, that he who has done this deed might be taken away from among you" (1 Cor. 5:2). Paul said the man should be removed from the church and explained why: "Do you not know that a little leaven leavens the whole lump?" (1 Cor. 5:6). Leaven is worked into dough and spreads throughout the batch, causing the entire loaf to take on the ability to rise. Paul compares unchecked, blatant, willful sin in our churches to leaven in bread.

I warned this pastor, "You are allowing sin to spread unchecked throughout your church. God will hold you accountable for the effect on the other sheep!" I went on, "A shepherd not only feeds the sheep but protects them as well. You like feeding them, but you are afraid of protecting them because you don't like confrontation. But both are important! You need to confront this man in a firm and loving way, and if he does not repent immediately, remove him from the church." If we don't feed sheep they

75

will starve, but if we don't protect them they will be devoured.

He and his wife turned white. She said, "I don't know if I want to be in ministry anymore. All I want to do is love people."

I answered, "It is convenient love, not true love, if you do not protect those people."

They admitted they were intimidated by some of the people in their church. They opened up and told me other problems. On the praise and worship team some of the musicians were disrespectful. I told them how frustrated I had been during the service, and now I knew why.

That night in the middle of my preaching a man interrupted to give a message in tongues. I asked him to stop, explaining that God does not interrupt Himself. The man understood and ceased speaking, but as he did the guitar player jumped up, shouting at me, "I'm not putting up with any more preaching from somebody who doesn't allow the Holy Spirit to move. I'm getting out of here!" He grabbed his wife and shouted to the bass player to come with him. The bass player, his wife and one other person stormed out. The atmosphere was thick with unrest; the congregation was bewildered.

I immediately asked the Holy Spirit what to do. He said, "Teach them about authority." As I taught, the peace of God came into the church as His order was established.

When I was finished, the Lord instructed me, "Tell the man you stopped to give the tongue and interpretation now."

A bit hesitant, I told the man I had corrected, "Sir, if you're able, I believe God wants you to give that message now."

He gave the message in tongues, and he also gave the interpretation.

It began, "Thus says the Lord, I have seen the infestation

of the sin in this church. I have only shown my servant a part of it. Heed his words, for they are My words."

I began to weep over the sin and rebellion permeating that church. The pastor was overwhelmed. Sin was rampant because the leaders were intimidated by the very ones God wanted them to care for.

I rejoiced to learn later that the pastor confronted the man and young woman who were living together. They both repented and made immediate plans to separate.

A Pastor Intimidated by His Own Board

Once I was ministering in another church where the meetings had begun Sunday morning and were scheduled to go through Wednesday night. We were having tremendous meetings, with evidence of repentance, healing and deliverance. The church had experienced a breakthrough in its finances. The attendance increased. But Tuesday evening before the service the pastor began to weep.

"What is wrong?" I asked.

"John, I am not jealous of you. I just do not understand why I never see God move. I am filled with the Holy Spirit, yet none of the gifts of the Spirit operate in my services. No one is healed or delivered, and everything just seems so difficult."

So I began to ask questions. It turned out there were two couples on his board who had both been filled with the Holy Spirit longer than he had. Because of this they told him what to do and how to run the church. I explained, "You're intimidated by your own board. You need to step back into your God given-authority and tell them you are the pastor — not them."

The next day he spoke with them. Both couples were upset and eventually left the church. The meetings were extended, and on the last evening a group of people came forward for prayer, but the Lord told me, "You are not to pray for these people. The pastor is."

I looked at the pastor, and I could see the power of God all over him. "Pastor," I said, "God says you are to pray for the people."

He began to run through the midst of that group of people. He would merely touch them and they would collapse under the power of God. There were some who fell before he touched them. The power of God was so strong that they were affected even before he got to them.

One girl who was demon-possessed was gloriously delivered. Within a few minutes everyone in that group of people was on the floor being ministered to by the Holy Spirit! The pastor turned, took one look at me and fell over backward on the floor. His wife had to close the service. A half-hour later two men picked him up off the floor. That church was never the same.

The power of God in the pastor was inactive because of intimidation. The result was that the presence and power of God were rare in his church. After breaking the power of this intimidation, the gift of God was released.

Same Story, Different Scene

I have witnessed this principle proven true in numerous churches as well as in the lives of individuals. I was ministering in a church overseas in which I could see clearly from the way the pastors and other leaders acted that they struggled with intimidation. Through the entire week I preached, encouraging them to stay strong in the spirit and press into their high calling in God. Four months after my departure the church had tripled in size! They moved out of their four-hundred-seat building and into an auditorium that sat two thousand. When I later returned to this nation the pastor told me that he and his church had not been the same since they broke through intimidation.

I was invited to minister for three days in Atlanta. On

the last night I preached on breaking the power of intimidation. The pastor was gloriously delivered from being intimidated by his own people. He said, "You have to come back immediately and stay for a week."

So I came back three weeks later, and we had nine services. God's power and presence were so strong that some people had to be carried out after midnight. People called the pastor at home in the middle of the night wondering what they should do, because some were still being touched by God's presence and power. They had never seen God move in such a powerful way.

This church had revival meetings every weekend for nine months after that. The pastor would call to tell me how powerful the services in his church were and what great things were happening in the lives of the members. He said no two meetings were the same. Their church grew from four hundred to seven hundred! He told me on several occasions that the night I preached on breaking intimidation was the turning point for his life and ministry.

I was in another "alive faith" church. The praise and worship could have put you to sleep. The pastor got up, made announcements and "taught" on the offering. It was as boring as anything I have ever sat through. As we ate after the service, all he could talk about was football and other unimportant things. Needless to say, it was a boring lunch!

The next night God had me preach on breaking intimidation. In the middle of the message this pastor fell to the floor, repenting of the weakness he had tolerated in his life and ministry. I knew God was doing a work in his life, but I didn't realize to what extent.

The next day he called. "John, my wife had one hour of sleep, and I didn't even go to bed!" he said. "We were up all night repenting and crying, then laughing. Then we would start all over again. Repent, cry, then laugh."

That day he went to his board and repented before them, apologizing for not being the leader God had called him to be. Eventually, a few of the board members left the church when they realized they could no longer control him. But the rest of his board joined with him and supported his growth.

The church and this man have never been the same. Now, four years later, the praise and worship is alive. They've had revival meetings every weekend for the past two years. When the pastor calls me, all he talks about is what God is doing and speaking through him and what's happening in his church. I have been back several times, and each time it gets better. He has also told me several times that this message was the turning point in his life and ministry.

This release is not only for pastors and leaders but for all believers as well. We have received many testimonies from individuals who have been liberated in every area of life by breaking out of the bondage of intimidation.

A woman attended a service at which I preached about breaking intimidation. Afterward, she said she felt the grip of fear and intimidation released from her life. A few nights later she and her daughter were held up at gunpoint in their driveway. The attackers grabbed the woman's purse, and the three young men quickly surrounded them.

Great boldness rose up inside her, and she began to speak in tongues as loudly as she could. The young man holding the gun yelled, "Stop that!" She didn't. The young men became so confused that her daughter was able to run into their house and call 911. The men ran, taking only her purse.

The next day a Christian man decided to walk to his mother's house on a different path than he normally took. He found this woman's purse in the woods and called her. The two of them rejoiced together. Only a small amount of cash was missing, and all her identification was still in her purse.

She told my wife she believed that message had imparted the courage that saved her life. In the past, she was so easily intimidated that she would have been overwhelmed by fear at such a confrontation. She was so excited to be free!

I give God all the glory for these testimonies. I too was bound by intimidation, but by His grace I am now free! This liberating wisdom and power to set captives free has come from Him.

We have identified fear and intimidation and their ability to hinder and, in most cases, stop the power and gift of God. However, our purpose is to go beyond just identification and move on to break its deadly grip!

Spiritual resistance
requires
spiritual assistance.

Chapter 7

THE SPIRIT
OF INTIMIDATION

In order to recognize and deal with intimidation we must be settled on two issues. First, fear, or timidity, is a spirit, and second, it is not from God.

> For God did not give us a *spirit* of timidity (2 Tim. 1:7, NIV, italics added).

The Greek word for *spirit* in this passage is *pneuma,* which is the same word used for the Holy Spirit or the spirit of man or a demon, according to Strong's concordance. Intimidation is not an attitude or a disposition. It is a *spirit.*

Since intimidation is a spirit it cannot be fought on the level of our intellect or will. Having a positive mental attitude will not overcome intimidation. Spiritual resistance requires spiritual assistance. It must be addressed in the realm of the spirit.

Consider this: Why would people who are intelligent and physically strong struggle with intimidation — often from someone or something weaker in body or mind? Perhaps everything is fine, but they live in constant dread that their circumstances might change for the worse. They spend all their time and energy worrying and trying to safeguard themselves against what may never happen. It is impossible for them to enjoy the present because they are so afraid of their future. It doesn't make sense, yet no matter how you reason with them, their fear persists. They have a spirit of timidity, or fear. They are not fighting natural weakness but spiritual weakness.

Next, consider men and women who always seem to get their way. Their stature or education doesn't matter. They may not hold any position of authority, yet those around them back down and yield to them. Why? It's simple. They control others by a spirit of intimidation. They have learned how to use intimidation to their advantage.

I ate breakfast with a man who owned a very prosperous business. He told me how he had lived and operated the business before he got saved. He explained, "I could get anything I wanted for my business by intimidating people. I literally could feel its power on me when I walked into city hall. I loved the fact that people were scared of me. I got whatever I wanted even from the city council." He had an intimidating spirit. The leaders of the city, even though they held positions of authority over him, dared not oppose him.

A Controlling Spirit

Elijah was not afraid of the nation of Israel when the Israelites were given over to Baal worship. What tremendous courage — one man against a nation! Nor was he frightened by the 850 false prophets. What resolve — one prophet against nearly a thousand religious leaders! He wasn't concerned in the least with the anger of the king of Israel either. All this would be more than most people could handle. However, he allowed one woman to intimidate him into running away and wanting to die! It doesn't make sense.

Psychologists might say he was afraid of women, but this would be a feeble argument at best because the nation of Israel was comprised of more than just men! No, this was a spiritual conflict of such magnitude that the nation, the king and the false prophets paled in comparison. Elijah faced in Jezebel a strong, controlling spirit of intimidation that the king and the false prophets did not have.

Let's find out what Scripture reveals about the nature of this spirit. Look at this exchange between Jehu and Jezebel's son, Joram.

> Now it happened, when Joram saw Jehu, that he said, "Is it peace, Jehu?" So he answered, "What peace, as long as the harlotries of your mother Jezebel and her *witchcraft* are so many?" (2 Kin. 9:22, italics added).

Do not stumble over the word *witchcraft*. Don't make the mistake of thinking of a woman with a wart on her nose flying around on a broom, casting spells and using potions. A person exercises witchcraft when he or she seeks to control. Yes, there is a form of witchcraft or control that conjures up demonic spirits. However, witchcraft is not limited to this. Paul rebuked the Galatian church, "O foolish Galatians! Who has bewitched you that you should not obey the truth" (Gal. 3:1). This bewitching was not from potions or spells. Paul was referring to teachers

85

who had persuaded them to disobey what God had clearly revealed to them. These teachers were not masters of the occult, but they did have a controlling spirit. And it had affected the entire church.

Jezebel had such a strong controlling and intimidating spirit that the king, the leaders and all the people of Israel gave way to her. Even Elijah yielded to it and ran for his life. When you let fear enter your heart, here are *some* of the things you stand to lose: peace, confidence, courage, endurance, heroism, resolution and security. The list goes on.

I have watched as people tried to rid themselves of fear's torment through positive thinking. They do not escape, for they are dealing with fear's effects, not its origin. You can pick the fruit off a tree, and for a while it will appear fruitless, but fruit will eventually grow back. The tree will continue to bear fruit until the roots are severed. So to break the power of intimidation, you must go after the spiritual force behind it.

Control and Intimidating Spirits in the Church

In our churches are those whose hearts are not right before God. They intimidate leadership to get what they want. They act submissive until things don't go their way. When the leadership is weak, they are the ones who run the church.

As I traveled to different churches, often I would face intimidation and not know why I was fighting it or where it was coming from. The reason: Intimidation is a spirit that gains expression through any person who will yield to it, even through a believer! The Bible admonishes believers not to give place to the devil (Eph. 4:27).

I am about to share a few experiences. I do so at the risk of being labeled "hyper-spiritual" or "demon paranoid." I realize some people look for a devil in every

86

problem they face. If you can blame a devil, you don't have to accept responsibility for your actions. Such an approach focuses more on devils than on Jesus. The Bible instructs us to keep our eyes on Jesus, not on devils. He is the author and finisher of our faith (Heb. 12:2).

The way I understand it, we are to live focused on Jesus, and if a devil gets in our way of doing this, we are to blast him with the Word of God and continue our pursuit of Jesus! Hallelujah! However, to break intimidation effectively we need to know it is a spirit which will not go away because it is ignored. Just the opposite occurs.

An Attack

I'm going to relate one of many incidents that confirms intimidation as a spirit. I was preaching a series of meetings at a church in the South. The first meeting was on a Sunday morning, and it was powerful. For years we used the tape of that service in one of our cassette series. After the service no one said anything intimidating or negative. In fact, the people around me were very positive. But later in the afternoon I found myself battling discouragement and confusion. I knew something was wrong but did not know where it was coming from. I had recognized these symptoms as the same I would fight when I came up against blatant intimidation. That night the Lord instructed me to preach on authority in the church, and many were ministered to.

After the service the pastor pulled me into his office. "You don't know how on target you were tonight in what you preached," he said. He proceeded to tell me how a female member of his church had called him that afternoon and said, "Pastor, I know you don't agree with what this man is preaching. He is too hard on the people. I know you will shut the meetings down after tonight because you're not like him. So I am not going to come tonight. I am going to stay home and pray against this man."

I now knew exactly where all the discouragement was coming from. I asked the pastor if he had corrected her. He is a very merciful man and told me that he did not. He said he told her to leave it in the Lord's hands. If this pastor had corrected her and stood in his authority I'm sure I would have had a different afternoon. What we do not confront will not change. If evil is ignored it becomes stronger! We both learned from that incident. The Lord used this experience to show me how to stay in my spiritual authority and not bow to a spirit of intimidation.

Thank God for the Holy Spirit who knew what was going on and had me confront that spirit from the pulpit — even though I did not know what was going on. The pastor knew, and it opened his eyes. Those meetings turned out to be some of the most powerful meetings of that entire year. I've returned to this church, and the pastor and I are now good friends.

Another Encounter With an Intimidating, Controlling Spirit

Another time I was asked to preach at a retreat overseas where almost a thousand people were registered. Two meetings were held each day and one in the evening. The first two services were very strong. I preached on holiness and repentance. Yet, in each service I could sense resistance in the atmosphere. After the second service I spent the entire afternoon in my room fighting heaviness and discouragement. I knew it was an intimidating, controlling spirit, but again no one had said anything contrary to me. But I had learned by this time that I wasn't wrestling with flesh and blood, but against evil spirits.

Believers need to learn to live in the spirit. The Spirit of God will reveal what you are up against. Without discernment we will focus our attention on the side effects. If I hadn't recognized what I was dealing with, I would have begun to wonder, Why am I fighting depression? Was I supposed to come? Why have I left my wife and children? Have I missed my calling? Should I stop traveling? If I had continued along these lines of thinking I would not have been fit to minister, and that was exactly what that intimidating, controlling spirit wanted. My focus would be on me, not on what God had for those people.

I struggled the entire afternoon. When I was picked up for the service that night I mentioned to my interpreter that I had battled intimidation all afternoon. My interpreter yelled, "Me too!" We discovered we had fought the same symptoms. That night I preached on the spirit of intimidation, and many were set free.

The next morning as I came to the pulpit, there was no anointing. God seemed silent. I stood on the platform for several minutes waiting to hear the word of the Lord. I prayed and had the people pray, but there was still no leading, unction or impression to do anything. Deep in my heart I knew I was in a battle. I realized the total focus of this attack was against me. I knew I had to break the words that had been spoken directly against me. God's Word says:

> No weapon formed against you shall prosper,
> and every tongue which rises against you in
> judgment you shall condemn. This is the heritage
> of the servants of the Lord, and their righteous-
> ness is from Me, says the Lord (Is. 54:17).

I began to break this attack of intimidation. I commanded every word spoken against me to be condemned. I did not care what the people thought. I have learned it is best to listen to my heart, where the Spirit speaks.

Immediately, the word of the Lord came to me like a

machine gun. God told me exactly what to have the people do. The power of God fell within two to three minutes. People were getting so filled with the Holy Spirit that they began to laugh uncontrollably. The move of God's Spirit was so strong that I didn't even preach. There were reports of people still in the auditorium at three in the afternoon. It was a great breakthrough, and my heart rejoiced. Had I not confronted that spirit it wouldn't have happened.

Later I learned from the interpreter that there was a female minister in the meetings who, after the schedule was set, came to the leader of the retreat and said, "Why should the people have to listen to John Bevere preach all the services of the retreat? We need other ministers to preach." She wanted to minister.

I had heard other unusual reports about this woman. She used unscriptural practices to minister "deliverance," such as administering eyedrops and rubbing wine on the skin. She had never been confronted. In fact, the leader permitted her to minister in a limited capacity during the retreat. Sad to say, leaders often choose to compromise rather than confront because they think it will be easier. But compromise is never easy — and is often costly.

After the meetings I spoke with the leader. I asked him if the reports I'd heard about this woman were true. He said they were. I shared my concern that she would question his choice of speakers after he had already determined God's direction for the retreat. I told him it showed she wanted to control him. (She was not a leader nor a member of his church.)

I asked him, "Why did you allow this woman to minister in the retreat?"

He said, "John, I told her she could not use those practices."

I explained, "You can stop her from using unscriptural

practices, but the spirit behind them is still there. The condition of her heart is no different. As the leader you wanted to maintain peace and consequently, you put a person with a controlling, intimidating spirit into a position of ministry and authority. That gave an intimidating spirit the legal right to fight against me and anyone else who did not agree with what it wanted."

To help him see what had happened, I shared an incident from my life. On one particular night when I was a college and career pastor, we had just experienced a powerful time of praise and worship. Tears flowed down the faces of many young people. God's peace and presence filled the room. We had been in worship for almost forty minutes. At that moment all were silent, with the exception of those crying softly.

All of a sudden a young man I'd never seen before spoke out in an unknown tongue. When he did, a disturbing, weird sensation hung over the room. Then the young woman next to him, whom I also had never seen before, came out with a strange interpretation.

Caught off guard because I had been enjoying the presence of the Lord from our praise and worship time, I did not say anything.

When she was finished, the atmosphere was different. The presence of the Lord was totally gone. I figured it was too late to say anything. The damage had already been done. So I asked everyone to sit down, made the weekly announcements and took the offering. Then I began to preach.

As I preached I thought, Where's the life? Where am I going? Why did I just say that? There was no anointing to preach, and I felt as if something were fighting me. I didn't understand why the gift of God was dormant, so I asked all the people to pray. The Lord spoke, "I want you to confront that man and woman."

I thought, It has already been twenty minutes. I can't do that. So I put aside what God had spoken and thought, I'll just pray a little longer. We kept praying and coming against spiritual opposition.

Several minutes later, in desperation, I said, "God, what is going on?"

I heard again in my spirit, "I want you to confront them."

Now it had been even longer. I thought, No way. People are going to think I am strange. We prayed ten more minutes, and there was no change. Discouraged, I dismissed the service.

I went home that night with a heavy heart. I did not even want to ask God about what happened. I just went to bed. The next morning I woke up feeling even heavier in my spirit. I went out to pray.

"God, what happened last night?" I asked.

He answered, "John, I told you to confront the man and woman." He went on, "When I put you into a position of leadership over a service [or anything else], you are responsible to maintain order and authority over that service. I will not do it, because I have entrusted it to you.

"When I put Adam in the garden, I told him to guard it. When the devil came to destroy, though I knew the severe consequence not only for Adam but the entire human race, I did not come down and knock the fruit out of his hand! I do not take back what I have given, and I had given him that responsibility. The man and woman I told you to confront had a rebellious spirit. When you did not confront them, that spirit was allowed to preside over the service. When this happened, My Spirit lifted because you gave your authority away."

I immediately repented, determining never to allow this to happen again.

After I told this story to this foreign pastor, he understood why he needed to confront the rebellious minister. His face lit up as the light of God's understanding entered his heart. I encouraged him, "As the shepherd of these people, you are not only called to feed them but also to protect them. Protection will mean confrontation."

I asked him, "Do you find yourself in situations where people ask something of you, and you know in your heart you should say no, but to maintain peace you say yes?"

He responded, "Yes, John, I do that." He then thought a moment and looked at me pensively. "That is hypocrisy, isn't it?"

I agreed. "You said that right, and this hypocrisy or compromise is born out of intimidation," I said.

He repented of having a timid spirit and left immediately to straighten things out with those he had been intimidated by. The next time I saw him there was a big smile on his face as he exclaimed, "I'm free!"

Realize that these examples of uncomfortable confrontation represent a few extreme situations. I have preached literally hundreds of services in which there was no resistance, but great liberty. Liberty is the norm; resistance, the exception. But I felt it necessary to present a few examples in great detail for your benefit.

Though these incidents deal with ministry, the principles apply to every area of life. Intimidation is a spirit and must be dealt with accordingly. If we try to fight spiritual battles with fleshly weapons, we will at best be frustrated, and at worst, wounded and defeated.

> For though we walk in the flesh, we do not war according to the flesh. For the weapons of our warfare are not carnal but mighty in God for pulling down strongholds, casting down arguments and every high thing that exalts itself

against the knowledge of God, bringing every thought into captivity to the obedience of Christ (2 Cor. 10:3-5).

The enemy of intimidation attacks our soul. It is not defeated through psychology or positive thinking. Our weapon against intimidation is the sword of the Spirit — standing firm on God's Word (Eph. 6:17)! As we'll see in the next chapter, confronting intimidation will wake up the gift of God inside of you.

BREAKING
INTIMIDATION

What can man do to me?

Chapter 8

STIR THE GIFT

The goal of intimidation is to make us give up our authority, thereby rendering our gifts inoperative. We are then reduced to operating in our own limited strength and ability. This usually changes our position from offensive to defensive. Then, aware that we are vulnerable, we further retreat to what is comfortable and safe.

Wake Up the Gift

So, if intimidation lulls the gift asleep, what wakes it up? The answer: *boldness*. Intimidation causes a person to draw back, while boldness lunges forward even in the face of opposition. How can an intimidated person apprehend boldness?

> For God has not given us a spirit of fear [intimidation], but of power and of love and of a sound mind (2 Tim. 1:7).

Boldness comes from the virtues of power, love and soundness of mind. Boldness is not a virtue in itself. We have all known people who were brazen and bold. True boldness comes from God and is fueled by godly virtue. Boldness that is fueled by God's character awakens the gifts in our lives.

Some people do not have virtue behind their boldness. They know the right things to say and act confident when faced with little or no opposition. But their strength does not run deep. It is superficial. Their bold face is a mask for arrogance or ignorance. Their roots are shallow, and eventually a strong enough storm will expose them. When the weather is good, you can't see how deeply a tree is rooted, but under the winds of adversity it will either be uprooted or proven strong.

Who's Stronger?

David said, "The Lord is the strength of my life; of whom shall I be afraid?" (Ps. 27:1). David declared the Lord his source of strength and power. Knowing there is none greater than God, he could fearlessly declare, "I fear no one!"

Not only did he boldly declare his confidence, he lived it as well. David knew the power of God because he knew God. This boldness enabled David to fulfill his destiny and rule righteously. Let's look at his younger years.

David was the eighth son of Jesse of Bethlehem. His three older brothers served in the army under King Saul. The Philistines had gathered their army against Israel. Daily their champion Goliath challenged the Israelite soldiers, "Choose a man for yourselves, and let him come down to me. If he is able to fight with me and kill me, then we will be your servants. But if I prevail against him and kill him, then you shall be our servants and serve us" (1 Sam. 17:8-9).

Ordinarily the Israelites might have considered this option over war, but Goliath was no regular soldier. According to some accounts he was ten-and-one-half feet tall. To put this in perspective, look at any basketball goal. His head would be a couple of inches above the rim! Not only was he big, he was an experienced warrior. His spearhead alone weighed fifteen pounds. His helmet was bronze, and he was sheathed in armor that weighed 125 pounds![1] The combined weight of his armor, spear and shield is estimated at over two hundred pounds, probably more than David weighed at the time. Needless to say, Goliath was very intimidating! The Bible says, "When Saul and all Israel heard these words of the Philistine, they were dismayed and greatly afraid" (1 Sam. 17:11).

Now David, who tended sheep, was sent by his father to bring supplies to his three older brothers and to see how they were faring. After giving the food to the supply keeper, he ran to meet his brothers. Soon the champion Goliath came out to taunt the Israelites for the fortieth day.

David was amazed by what he saw — not the size of Goliath, but the reaction of his brothers and countrymen. "All the men of Israel, when they saw the man, fled from him and were dreadfully afraid" (1 Sam. 17:24). David must have wondered, Have they forgotten who's on our side? He is not challenging us. He is challenging God!

So David boldly demanded, "Who is this uncircumcised Philistine, that he should defy the armies of the living God?" (1 Sam. 17:26). The air was thick with confrontation. His older brothers felt naked as David exposed their intimidation. They did not want to hear their little brother make such a statement. It brought out in the open their weakness, which up to that time they did not have to face. They had been silent by mutual agreement based on compromise.

They lashed out at David, knowing that if they could discredit him, it would cover their shame. Big brother, who was intimidated by Goliath, tried to intimidate little brother.

> When Eliab, David's oldest brother, heard him speaking with the men, he burned with anger at him and asked, "Why have you come down here? And with whom did you leave those few sheep in the desert? I know how conceited you are and how wicked your heart is; you came down only to watch the battle" (1 Sam. 17:28, NIV).

Eliab was now bold — bold with anger. He attacked David's character, not the problem facing Israel. When a person is intimidated, he looks for an escape, a release of pressure. If he is weak, he will make excuses. If he is strong, he will often attack those who have confronted him by putting some form of blame back on them.

Notice Eliab accused David of conceit and wickedness. Because Eliab thought only of himself, he assumed David was the same way. But David was not. He was a man after God's heart. He was not proud but humble before the Lord.

People who have strong personalities will use intimidation to make a lie look like the truth. You must stay in the spirit to overcome the strength of such attacks.

Perhaps Eliab was jealous. Samuel anointed David as king, even though Eliab was the eldest. He seemed to have the characteristics of a great leader and warrior. Even Samuel, upon seeing Eliab, thought, Surely the Lord's anointed is before me! But God used this to teach Samuel a lesson: "Do not look at his appearance or at his physical stature, because I have refused him. For the Lord does not see as man sees; for man looks at the outward appearance, but the Lord looks at the heart" (1 Sam. 16:7).

So whose heart was proud? God revealed to Samuel that He would not choose Eliab based on his stature or appearance, nor would He reject him on those factors. God judges the heart. When God finds pride in a heart, He resists that person (James 4:6). God rejected Eliab because he was proud in heart. So Eliab possessed the very thing that he accused David of — pride!

Usually intimidation will accuse you of the very weakness it seeks to hide. Those who act pure outwardly but have an impure heart will always attack the pure in heart. Remember that pure-hearted Timothy was intimidated. I'm sure there were men and women in the church at Ephesus whose hearts were as corrupt as Eliab's.

Jesus constantly faced intimidation. The impure Pharisees and lawyers tried to discredit Him or catch Him in His words. If they could only intimidate Him, then they could control Him. So they said He was a traitor, a glutton, a drunkard and a demon-possessed sinner, which were the very characteristics many of them possessed. By refusing to come under their control, Jesus exposed their hearts.

Why do the impure seek to intimidate the pure? To relieve themselves of conviction and to maintain control. If successful, they don't have to examine their hearts and repent. Eliab knew that his discrediting and intimidating attack would bring his brother David under his submission and deflect the pressure off himself.

The tables were turned; David was the one being confronted. He was under attack, and his big brother was much larger than he was. Remember, big brothers can make things uncomfortable for little ones. If David did not do what Eliab wanted, he might have a lot of trouble at home later. He might have to pay many times over for upholding truth. Would it be worth it?

That wasn't the only pressure against him. Everyone there was backing Eliab. They did not want their fears to be exposed by a ruddy kid either! It would have been easier for David to back off and not pursue it any further. This was exactly what Eliab, the intimidator, and the others wanted.

David chose to side with God, breaking the intimidation launched against him. He asked Eliab, "What have I done now? Is there not a cause?" (1 Sam. 17:29). He was actually saying, Is what I said not true? Where is your courage? I am not afraid. It is obvious that since you all have been afraid for the past forty days that God had to find someone who would not be intimidated and who would fight this uncircumcised Philistine! There is a cause for me being here.

He then was brought before the king. Saul, who was also intimidated by Goliath, reasoned with David. "You are not able to go against this Philistine to fight with him; for you are a youth, and he a man of war from his youth" (1 Sam. 17:33). Although this was not as barbed as his older brother's statement, it still was a belittling comment given to the young man by the intimidated king.

David responded to the king differently from how he responded to his older brothers. He said,

> "Your servant used to keep his father's sheep, and when a lion or a bear came and took a lamb out of the flock, I went out after it and struck it, and delivered the lamb from its mouth; and when it arose against me, I caught it by its beard, and struck and killed it. Your servant has

killed both lion and bear; and this uncircumcised Philistine will be like one of them, seeing he has defied the armies of the living God." Moreover David said, "The Lord, who delivered me from the paw of the lion and from the paw of the bear, He will deliver me from the hand of this Philistine" (1 Sam. 17:34-37).

With his brothers and soldiers he was very bold and confrontational. However, when he spoke to the king, he knew he was addressing one who was in authority over him. He entreated the king as a son would his father. He presented his experience and cited the Lord as his Deliverer, believing the king would see accurately.

The responsibility and accountability for this decision rested with the king. If the battle was lost, a nation would go into bondage. David knew that if he was supposed to fight, God would turn the king's heart. It is important that we behave in this manner with those in authority over us. After David's speech, Saul agreed to let him fight. "Go," he said, "and the Lord be with you."

David refused the protection of Saul's armor. Placing himself under the protection of the Lord, David's Shield and Buckler, he took up his staff in one hand and sling in the other and went to the brook to get five smooth stones. When the Philistine approached, David faced his biggest challenge in overcoming intimidation. This time if he was intimidated it would not only cause the gift of God to lie dormant, but it would cost him his life and bring his country into bondage.

And when the Philistine looked about and saw David, he disdained [belittled] him; for he was only a youth, ruddy and good-looking. So the Philistine said to David, "Am I a dog, that you come to me with sticks?" And the Philistine cursed David by his gods. And the Philistine said to David, "Come to me, and I will give your flesh to the birds of the air and the beasts of the field!" (1 Sam. 17:42-44).

Goliath tried to intimidate David not only with his size, but also with his words. After cursing David, this giant painted a vivid picture of what he intended to do to him. Clearly outmatched, David never doubted the source of his strength or weaponry:

> Then David said to the Philistine, "You come to me with a sword, with a spear, and with a javelin. But I come to you in the name of the Lord of hosts, the God of the armies of Israel, whom you have defied. This day the Lord will deliver you into my hand, and I will strike you and take your head from you. And this day I will give the carcasses of the camp of the Philistines to the birds of the air and the wild beasts of the earth, that all the earth may know that there is a God in Israel. Then all this assembly shall know that the Lord does not save with sword and spear; for the battle is the Lord's, and He will give you into our hands" (1 Sam. 17:45-47).

David boldly declares the faithfulness of God. The men of Israel had only seen how big the giant was, but David saw how big God was! The men of Israel watched as David *ran* toward God's enemy — not only confident in speech but also in action.

> Then David put his hand in his bag and took out a stone; and he slung it and struck the Philistine in his forehead, so that the stone sank into his forehead, and he fell on his face to the earth (1 Sam. 17:49).

David's boldness was contagious, and Israel's hope was restored. God was on their side, while the Philistines had only a dead champion. The Israelites attacked and pursued the Philistines, defeating them.

Three times during this event David faced intimidation. First, his brothers and fellow soldiers tried their best to belittle, slander and discourage him. If he would have come under their intimidation, he would have backed off from pursuing what God had put in his heart. He would have turned around and gone home, and the gift of God would have been dormant. The results would have been much different: The giant would not have been killed by David. He would have continued to oppress the nation, and God would have had to find another man to do His work.

Second, he faced discouraging and belittling statements from the king. If David had backed down, the gift of God would have stayed dormant. But he refused to be intimidated by even the king. He kept his respect for his nation's leader but was able to persuade the king to allow him to fight.

Third, he faced intimidation from the Philistine giant. Not only was his size overwhelming to the natural eye, but this man was very confident. He attempted to make David feel as if he were insignificant and weaker than a small animal. If he would have come under his intimidation, the gift of God in him would have remained dormant, and it would have cost him his life.

David was so confident in God's power that he was able to put his life on the line. This boldness woke up the gift of God in him, and he defeated the giant who intimidated and oppressed the entire army forty days!

The Power of the New Covenant

In Paul's letter to the Corinthian church, he compared the glory of the ministry of death (the old covenant) with the glory of ministry of the Spirit (the new covenant, 2 Cor. 3:7-8). He reasoned that if the power of the old was so glorious that the children of Israel could not look steadily at the face of Moses, then how much more powerful is the ministry of the new and life-giving covenant!

Paul described the "new" as "this treasure in earthen vessels, that the excellence of the power may be of God and not of us" (2 Cor. 4:7). Here is another man who knew his God and realized a strength or power that was not his own. Paul continued:

> For if what is passing away was glorious, what remains is much more glorious. Therefore, since we have such hope, we use great boldness of speech (2 Cor. 3:11-12).

This power breeds boldness. You find great boldness in believers who don't trust in their own strength. They are not intimidated by circumstance, person or devil, because God is not. This is our promise in Hebrews 13:5-6:

> For He [the Lord] Himself has said, "I will never leave you nor forsake you." So we may boldly say: "The Lord is my helper; I will not fear. What can man do to me?"

We need to declare boldly: *What can man do to me?*

This same confidence is available to every believer. Why are we called believers if we will not believe? Believe what? Believe God! No man or devil has the right to intimidate a true believer. Why? Because of Jesus. No name is higher; no power is greater. In His words, "Behold! I have given you authority and power...over all the power that the enemy [possesses]; and nothing shall in any way harm you" (Luke 10:19, AMP).

Could it be clearer? He has given his people power over *all* the enemy possesses. Intimidation is an enemy. It lies to you and says, I have more authority or power than you. You had better back off and do what I say! If you don't, you'll pay the consequences.

If we listen to these intimidating lies, the gift of God will go dormant, and we will live in an oppressed state. But when we know the One who has promised to be faithful, we can rest in the power that is above all other powers and, with David, face our giant of intimidation with great boldness.

Is Your Faith So Complex You Can't Believe?

These truths are not hard to understand. In fact, they're simple. The true gospel is not complicated. People fall short because of unbelief.

Ask yourself and answer honestly: Does your confidence rest in what God has said or in what you see and experience? If you measure everything by what has happened in your past, you will never grow beyond it.

Do you base your belief on what you see happen to others? Is your level of trust gauged by the faithfulness of others?

If you answered yes to these questions, then probe deeper. Have you complicated things by trying to explain past failures — yours or other's? Complex faith does not kill giants. It imprisons us in "wonder" land where we try to figure out what we cannot change and hesitate to make any move.

Why can't we believers just believe? Why do we allow our insecurities to complicate the gospel?

I want to share with you something I will never forget. The year was 1980, and I was a student living in North Carolina. I awoke at four o'clock in the morning out of a sound sleep to the sound of my own voice screaming,

"I'm just looking for someone to believe!"

It jolted me. The bed was drenched with sweat. I knew that God had spoken to me in an unusual and supernatural way.

At the time I thought, How obvious. Why didn't God give me something profound? Of course I know He needs people to believe!

The next morning the words swam in my head. Over and over I heard the whisper, "I'm just looking for someone to believe; I'm just looking for someone to believe." As I listened again, I realized He had not shown me something trivial, but the very key to walking with God!

I pored over the Gospels, noting that Jesus grieved over and was frustrated by people's unbelief. When His disciples couldn't cast the devil out of a young man, Jesus sharply rebuked them for it.

> Then Jesus answered and said, "O faithless and perverse generation, how long shall I be with you? How long shall I bear with you? Bring him here to Me" (Matt. 17:17).

What a thing to say to your own disciples! Jesus wasn't wishy-washy like so many leaders are today! He made it clear to them that the gift of God would remain dormant in them if they could not believe. He wanted it known that He was grieved with them.

I also noticed what delighted Jesus: those who believe without question! A Gentile Roman soldier got more attention for his faith than anyone else in Israel. This Roman told Jesus that He did not even need to come to his home, that if He only spoke a word his servant would be healed. "When Jesus heard it, He marveled, and said to those who followed, 'Assuredly, I say to you, I have not found such great faith, not even in Israel!'" (Matt. 8:10).

We want Jesus to come to our house, but we're going to question Him when He gets there. We've made faith so difficult. So, what is faith? Believing God will do what He has said He will.

Jesus said He gave us power and authority over all the

power of the enemy. All we need to do is believe Him and then walk in that power and authority. We don't need to complicate our walk with fear, doubt or reminders of our past shortcomings and failures. If we do, we are robbed of our boldness, and we become unable to step out in God's ability. The gift of God in us will lie dormant!

Before we confidently step out of our boat into the stormy waters of life, we must know the motives of our hearts, lest we sink! The next chapter will show you the difference between a motive that will help you stand and one that will make you sink.

*It is easy to be confident
as long as God is doing
what we expect.*

Chapter 9

THE ROOT
OF INTIMIDATION

Walking free from intimidation has nothing to do with being an extrovert. Some of the most outgoing people I have known have battled intimidation. As a matter of fact, sometimes their exuberance is merely a cover-up for the timidity they fight within themselves. Shutting down is not the only symptom of being intimidated. With some people, the more uncomfortable they are, the more they talk.

Being able to be intimidated has nothing to do with how anointed you are either. I have known men who were powerful in ministry, yet struggled with intimidation. When the anointing rested on them they were fearless, their weakness cloaked in God's anointing. Yet when the mantle of anointing was lifted, there remained only a man battling fear and insecurity. In one-on-one situations their timidity was shockingly apparent. How do I know this to be true? Because I was such a man.

You can be outgoing, strong, bold — even anointed — and still fight intimidation. When the pressure becomes strong enough, what you're made of is exposed. Possessing a spirit of timidity has nothing to do with a deficiency in personality, physical strength or anointing. So, what does render people vulnerable to intimidation?

Appearance vs. Truth

In answer, observe Simon Peter. He was outgoing, never shy to voice his opinion. He was bold. By all appearances, Peter was strong-willed and fearless. It seemed nothing could intimidate Peter, but something did. His fear of death caused him to deny Jesus three times. So the ability to walk free from intimidation is not a function of a strong personality, or Simon would have been the least likely to deny Jesus and the most equipped to remain faithful.

Some have a tendency to dismiss Simon Peter as all talk; they say that when it came time for action he was really "chicken." In answer to this I ask, "How many chickens would dare to stand up to a fully-armed mob with guards and make an offensive attack?" Peter boldly did! John 18:3,10 records:

> Then Judas, having received a detachment of troops, and officers from the chief priests and Pharisees, came there with lanterns, torches, and weapons...Then Simon Peter, having a sword, drew it and struck the high priest's servant, and cut off his right ear.

This doesn't sound like a chicken to me. So why would

Simon Peter defy the soldiers, only to cower before a servant girl? Yes, that's right. It was a servant girl who intimidated him! "Now Peter sat outside in the courtyard. And a servant girl came to him, saying, 'You also were with Jesus of Galilee.' But he denied it" (Matt. 26:69-70).

Why the change?

A Bold Front

To answer, let's go back to earlier that evening. All the disciples were together celebrating Passover. Jesus warned them, "All of you will be made to stumble because of Me this night" (Matt. 26:31). But Peter made himself an exception and boldly declared, "Even if all are made to stumble because of You, I will never be made to stumble" (Matt. 26:33). What a valiant display of courage. It looked as if Jesus must have been mistaken when he included Peter in that number.

But Jesus looked straight into the soul of Peter and corrected him, "Assuredly I say to you that this night, before the rooster crows, you will deny Me three times" (v. 34). What a blow to Peter's confidence! Jesus told Peter that not only would he stumble, but he would deny Him also.

A man weak in personality or will would have backed down at this point. Had the Master ever been wrong? But Peter further defended his position, "Even if I have to die with You, I will not deny You!" (v. 35). In fact, this bold declaration inspired the others to agree: "And so said all the disciples" (v. 35).

Motives Can Be Different From Appearances

On the surface it appeared that these men had great courage and pure motives. On closer inspection we find something other than the love of God motivating them.

Before Jesus warned them, He shared with them,

113

"Behold, the hand of My betrayer is with Me on the table" (Luke 22:21). How horrible, how terrible, to think one of them could betray Jesus. One who had lived and walked with Him all this time, one He had cared for, would now raise his heel against Him — the Messiah!

Although Jesus knew, and had known from the beginning who it was and what he would do, this is the first His disciples had heard of it. Can you imagine the dread and suspicion that hung over the room after this announcement?

"They began to question among themselves, which of them it was who would do this thing" (Luke 22:23). They were confused and in disbelief that one of them could be capable of such an unthinkable act of wickedness. So what was their motive for this investigation? Surely it must have been concern for Jesus. But was it? Their conversation gives them away. Look at the very next verse:

> Now there was also a dispute among them, as to which of them should be considered the greatest (Luke 22:24).

As we can clearly see, their reason for the inquest was selfishness and pride. Jesus told them He was about to be turned over to the chief priests to be condemned to death, and the disciples started jockeying for power and position. What selfishness!

We can guess who led the dispute. More than likely it was Simon Peter acting consistently with his past displays of leadership and with his dominating personality.

Perhaps he was quick to remind the others how he had been the only one brave enough to walk on water (Matt. 14:28-31). Or maybe he refreshed their memory about his figuring out who Jesus really was (Matt. 16:15-16), topping it off with a rehearsal of his experience on the mount of transfiguration with Jesus, Moses and Elijah (Matt. 17:1-8).

He was quite possibly confident he had proved himself the greatest of the twelve. But was this confidence rooted in love? I'm sure Peter thought it was at the time. Yet it would appear otherwise later. His confidence was anchored in pride and selfishness. Keeping this in mind, we'll move on.

The Oil Press

"Then Jesus came with them to a place called Gethsemane, and said to the disciples, 'Sit here while I go and pray over there'" (Matt. 26:36).

The word *Gethsemane* literally means an "oil press."[1] An oil press extracts oil from the olive. The olive does not freely yield oil. Only when great pressure is applied will the oil from within come out. Gethsemane is the place of such pressure — not on olives, but on hearts. Under intense pressure what is inside us will come out, often to our own surprise. In other words, the motives of your heart are tried and exposed when trials (pressures) come.

As Jesus went into Gethsemane with Peter, James and John, the Scriptures say, "He began to be sorrowful and deeply distressed" (Matt. 26:37). Jesus' soul was "exceedingly sorrowful" because He was in the oil press. He was fighting His greatest battle — the temptation to fulfill the will of the Father in another way and thereby save Himself.

Some people do not believe Jesus was capable of sin. We must remember, Jesus was tempted "in all points as we are, yet without sin" (Heb. 4:15). To be tempted means something had to be wrestled with. Jesus was not automatically immune to the struggles, just always triumphant over them. Why? Because He did not exercise His own will. If it had been impossible for Him to sin, then it would have been impossible to be tempted. This does not diminish His glory but further illustrates how worthy He is because He did not sin. Hallelujah!

This was Jesus' request in the garden: "O My Father, if it

is possible, let this cup pass from Me; nevertheless, not as I will, but as You will" (Matt. 26:39).

This is the first time we see the will of the Father and the will of the Son in conflict in the life of Jesus. Up until the garden they were so intermingled that we only saw the will of the Father manifested through the life of Jesus. But the overwhelming pressure of this battle raged in His soul. It exposed the only thing that could hold Him back — choosing to fulfill the will of the Father another way and thereby saving Himself. Earlier Jesus told the Pharisees His life was His own to lay down (John 10:17-18). God did not force Him to do this. That is why He wrestled — alone.

He had known this struggle was before Him long before He knelt in the garden. He had shared it with His disciples three times before they came to Jerusalem. He told them it was the will of His Father that He suffer, die and rise from the dead.

A few days earlier He confided to His disciples, "Now My soul is troubled, and what shall I say? 'Father, save Me from this hour'? But for this purpose I came to this hour. Father, glorify Your name" (John 12:26-27).

Jesus was willing to lay down His own life at the feet of death so that the name of the Father would be glorified. He had just shared this principle with His disciples, "He who loves his life will lose it, and he who hates his life in this world will keep it for eternal life" (John 12:25).

This scripture holds two answers — why Peter couldn't follow through with what he had vowed and why Jesus could. Jesus loved His Father more than His own life, so He could lay His life down. Peter thought he loved Jesus more than his own life, but the oil press of Gethsemane exposed his motives.

In the garden it was not enough that Jesus knew the will of the Father. He now had to become it. This was so difficult that He asked His Father if there were any other way. In prayer, He fervently battled this temptation of self-preservation and resisted to the point of sweating blood (Luke 22:44).

Jesus' power to resist temptation was rooted in what He loved and didn't love. He lost Himself in the love for His Father (John 14:31). This love would conquer what no man had conquered before: the love of self! Oil broke forth, proving His love for His Father not only in word, but also in sacrifice and obedience.

Now looked at how the "press" or pressure affected Peter and the other disciples.

Willing Spirit, Weak Flesh

After Jesus had battled His will for an hour, He rose up and went to His disciples only to find them "sleeping from sorrow" (Luke 22:45). The disciples were no longer debating who was the greatest. They were heavy with grief and sadness. Jesus was not the only one under pressure. His disciples were in the oil press as well!

They were facing the temptation to save themselves. Yet they had no strength to draw upon because they focused on their own wills, not the will of the Father. Unlike Jesus, they had no desire to bring their focus back to God's will. If we count our own lives dear, we will not fight just to be able to give them up.

Think of it: While Jesus battled to lose His life, the disciples avoided the fight by sleeping. Jesus spoke specifically to Peter, "What? Could you not watch with Me one hour? Watch and pray, lest you enter into temptation. The spirit indeed is willing, but the flesh is weak" (Matt. 26:40-41).

There was Peter, this man of bold promises, sleeping instead of praying. He had not yet learned to draw on a strength that was not his own, so he protected what he thought was his strength by sleeping.

Our spirits, or hearts, may be willing, but our flesh will always seek to protect itself. Consequently, if our flesh is not crucified, we will give it what it wants. Peter wanted to be faithful to Jesus but couldn't because his flesh overpowered him. He loved his own life more than he desired God's will. He did not recognize the true condition of his heart. He had meant what he had said and truly believed he would sacrifice his life for Jesus. However, out of the "press" came what was foreshadowed at the Last Supper: selfishness and pride.

Two Different Outcomes

After Jesus found the disciples sleeping, He went away a second time to pray. When He returned, He found them asleep again, for "their eyes were heavy" (Matt. 26:43). Even after Jesus warned them, they could not rouse themselves. "So He left them, went away again, and prayed the third time, saying the same words. Then He came to His disciples and said to them, 'Are you still sleeping and resting? Behold, the hour is at hand'" (vv. 44-45).

Jesus prayed for three hours until He knew His battle was won. His will was totally one with the Father's. He was now ready to face the intimidation of the enemy at the hands of the Jewish leaders and Roman soldiers.

Jesus' ability to stand firm even in the heat of persecution amazed the Roman governor. "And while He was being accused by the chief priests and elders, He answered nothing. Then Pilate said to Him, 'Do You not hear how many things they testify against You?' But He answered him not one word, so that the governor marveled greatly" (Matt. 27:12-14).

Boldness is not how loudly or how much we talk. It is also found in silence — silence while false accusations are thrown in your face. Jesus stayed in His authority by not reacting. He knew they had no power over Him. To react would indicate they did. They attempted to control Jesus with their accusations, threats and powerful positions. To answer them would be folly, for they had no concern for the truth. Jesus knew they couldn't take His life because He had already given it to the Father!

As Jesus faced His accusers, Peter warmed himself by the fire just outside. Intimidated by the mere servants of those leaders, Peter denied even knowing Jesus (Matt. 26:69-75). Even though Peter said he would die before denying Jesus, he ended up becoming intimidated and doing exactly what he said he would not do. The reason: He loved his own life.

His words to Jesus showed great love for Him, but his actions spoke louder. This love for himself was the root of his timidity. It was well hidden behind the bold statements and actions he made earlier, but the oil press revealed his timid spirit.

The root of fear and intimidation is the love of self. Perfect love casts out fear and gives us boldness. Boldness born of love breaks the grip of intimidation. Imperfect love, or self-love opens the door to intimidation.

> Love has been perfected among us in this: That we may have boldness in the day of judgment.[2] There is no fear in love; but perfect love casts out fear, because fear involves torment. But he who fears has not been made perfect in love (1 John 4:17-18).

Fear and intimidation are magnified as we focus on ourselves. Torment cries, "What about me? What will happen to me?"

Jesus said, "Greater love has no one than this, than to lay down one's life..." (John 15:13). When we truly lay down our lives out of love for Jesus, we will no longer care what happens to us because we know we are committed into His care. Then we are dead and hidden in Him. We do not need to worry because our lives are no longer our own, but His. He purchased us; therefore, whatever happens to us is His concern only. We just love and obey.

Fear should no longer torment us because a dead person can't be tormented. You can point a gun at a man in a casket and threaten him, but he won't even blink.

What About Everyone Else?

What about the rest of the disciples? They are joined in with Peter, professing they would die before denying Jesus. How did they fare in the oil press? They fled even before Peter did. The Bible reports that when they saw the soldiers take Jesus, "all the disciples forsook Him and fled" (Matt. 26:56).

They were all afraid for themselves. They too had slept rather than prayed. At their last meal with Him, they had fought over who was the greatest among them. It was as if they weren't listening or could not listen. They could only hear: What will happen to me? Their love of self was revealed in the oil press.

Their motives were no different from Peter's. Peter was just in a more difficult situation because he followed the soldiers to where they took Jesus.

All Boldness Is Not Motivated by Love

You may still wonder what gave Peter the boldness to stand sword-in-hand before a small army. I believe his boldness was drawn from the approval of others. He thrived on impressing others. Think about it. There had just been a debate over who was the greatest. (This was not the first time this subject had come up. The disciples were in constant competition.) This was fresh in Peter's mind, and now he was given the opportunity to prove his great faithfulness.

But as he sat by the fire with the servants of the high priest, no longer surrounded by his peers, his true insecurities surfaced. The fear normally hidden by his outgoing personality was exposed.

Previous incidents also revealed Peter's faltering boldness. One was when Peter walked on water. While all the other disciples watched, Peter yelled, "Lord, if it is You, command me to come to You on the water" (Matt. 14:28). Peter got out of the boat and walked on the sea. Perhaps his boldness was fueled by impressing his peers. However, alone in the middle of a boisterous sea, he cried out for Jesus to save him. As he walked through the waves, he realized none of his competitors was alongside him. Under pressure he called for Jesus to bail him out.

It is quite probable that Peter thought Jesus would bail him out of this incident in the garden just as He had many times before. And he was right. But what Peter and all the others did not expect was to see Jesus arrested. Even though Jesus told them repeatedly this would happen, they still believed He would establish His kingdom on earth now (Acts 1:6; Matt. 16:21).

It is easy to be confident as long as God is doing what we expect. But when He surprises, we can falter. Something happens in our lives or ministries that catches us unaware, and we lose our boldness. Often we are not prepared to suffer affliction, persecution or trials. Like children, we are comfortable with routine and our own way. When we don't get what we want when we want it and the way we want it, our hearts are tested. If we are hit with trials, our hearts are weighed. We may appear confident when God gives us exactly what we want or when life is predictable, but when things go differently, our motives are revealed. Jesus describes this condition:

These likewise are the ones sown on stony ground who, when they hear the word, immediately receive it with gladness; and they have no root in themselves, and so endure only for a time. Afterward, when tribulation or persecution arises for the word's sake, immediately they stumble (Mark 4:16-17).

Notice that the reason they did not endure is that they did not have roots. How do we develop roots that will hold us firm? What are we to be rooted in? Ephesians 3:17 says that we are to be rooted and grounded in our love for Christ. True love does not seek its own. People whose love is without roots endure as long as it is easy for them. They have not been crucified with Christ, but have come to Jesus for what they can get, not for who He is!

Those who truly love seek nothing but their Beloved and what pleases Him. Love does not hold expectations. Rather, it gives. This motive remains unaffected when things turn out to be different from what is expected. Love will not become discouraged (lose courage), so it will not be intimidated.

The boldness it takes to break the power of intimidation must be fueled by our love for God. "For God has not given us a spirit of fear [intimidation], but of power and of love and of a sound mind" (2 Tim. 1:7). Power is a part of breaking intimidation, but it is not enough by itself. As I have already said, I have seen anointed men buckle under intimidation during times of pressure.

Just having a sound mind is not enough either. It had been revealed to Peter by the Holy Spirit that Jesus was the Messiah (Matt. 16:13-18). It was only when Peter was filled with the love of God that he would truly lay down his life. We will look at this in the next chapter.

The only way
to conquer intimidation
is to lose your life.

Chapter 10

DESIRE IS NOT ENOUGH

Good intentions are not enough. Peter wanted to show he could be loyal even if it meant death. But the strength of this desire was not enough to keep it. The fear in his heart overcame his love for the Master. Jesus addressed this head on after His resurrection.

John chapter 21 tells us that Jesus appeared to His disciples and prepared fish and bread for their breakfast. He then asked Peter three times, "Do you love me?" The first two times Jesus used the word *agapao*, which emphasizes action involved with love. But Peter answered back each time with the Greek word *phileo*. This word is limited to the affections or feelings of love, independent of action.

Peter was grieved when Jesus questioned him a third time. This third time Jesus used the word *phileo*. Jesus reduced the love in question to the level of affection rather than action. In frustration Peter answered, "Lord, You know all things; You know that I love You" (John 21:17), meaning, "You know I have affection for You."

Jesus started by asking essentially, "Do you love me enough to lay down your life?" This illustrates the love described by the word *agapao*. Peter answered truthfully and humbly that his love was an emotional, or affectionate, love. Remember, he had just denied Jesus. He recognized his own weakness. His affectionate love alone was not strong enough for him to lay down his life.

Finally Jesus asked Peter, "Do you love Me affectionately?" The reason: Jesus knew Peter was now a broken man who was not yet capable of *agapao* love.

Jesus, wanting to explain to Peter what He meant when He questioned him the first two times, said, "'Most assuredly, I say to you, when you were younger, you girded yourself and walked where you wished; but when you are old, you will stretch out your hands, and another will gird you and carry you where you do not wish.' This He spoke, signifying by what death he would glorify God. And when He had spoken this, He said to him, 'Follow Me'" (John 21:18-19).

I believe Jesus was telling Peter, "You failed before in the strength of affectionate love, but there is coming a day when you will face your greatest fear and be victorious in the strength of perfected love." Up until that point Peter had loved to the best of human ability, but that had failed him. This time as Peter followed Jesus he would be equipped with *agapao*. That kind of love is not born out of man's desire for it but is shed abroad in our hearts by the Father (Rom. 5:5). God's love (*agape*, or *agapao*) is not afraid to die for another.

Jesus encouraged Peter, telling him that when he faced the "press" again he would come forth victorious. He would be able to fulfill what he had previously vowed in presumption: He would die before denying Jesus. With the grip of fear and intimidation released, Peter would be a changed man.

God does this for our benefit. He will strengthen us when we are intimidated. He will allow us to face repeatedly what we fear until we are victorious. When we come to the end of our strength, we will cry out for His. In this strength we cannot fail because love never fails (1 Cor. 13:8). God does not want us running from our areas of weakness. He wants us to face them fearlessly.

Please Take This Away!

Paul knew this well. "And lest I should be exalted above measure by the abundance of the revelations, a thorn in the flesh was given to me, a messenger of Satan to buffet me, lest I be exalted above measure" (2 Cor. 12:7).

The word for *messenger* in Greek refers to an angelic being (see Strong's concordance). I believe this verse refers to an evil angel that Satan sent to buffet Paul. This being stirred up problems for Paul everywhere he went. Second Corinthians 11:24-27 records some of the problems Paul encountered:

> From the Jews five times I received forty stripes minus one. Three times I was beaten with rods; once I was stoned; three times I was shipwrecked; a night and a day I have been in the deep; in journeys often, in perils of waters, in perils of robbers, in perils of my own countrymen, in perils of the Gentiles, in perils in the city, in perils in the wilderness, in perils in the sea, in perils among false brethren; in weariness and toil, in sleeplessness

often, in hunger and thirst, in fastings often, in cold and nakedness.

Everywhere he preached he ran into intense persecution for the gospel. Chains and tribulations awaited him in every city. He was whipped, beaten with rods, stoned, shipwrecked, robbed and more. So he went to God about it.

> Concerning this thing I pleaded with the Lord three times that it might depart from me (2 Cor. 12:8).

Understandably, he wanted to be free from this resistance and persecution. God answered:

> My grace is sufficient for you, for My strength is made perfect in weakness (2 Cor. 12:9a).

The Lord was essentially saying, "Paul, don't ask Me to remove these things, but rather ask that My grace and strength will raise you above what you cannot handle. Paul, where there are no obstacles, there is no need for power. A victory can occur only where there is a battle. The greater the battle, the greater the victory. A true soldier does not run from conflict but runs to it."

In the heat of battle is not the time to ask God to take us out of the war. It is the time to pray for His grace so we may triumph in it. God is glorified when we face something impossible to overcome in our human strength. It is then that His strength rests on us for all to see. God's grace conquers every fear and obstacle we face! Encourage yourself with a few of God's exhortations:

> Now thanks be to God who always leads us in triumph in Christ (2 Cor. 2:14).

> But thanks be to God, who gives us the victory through our Lord Jesus Christ (1 Cor. 15:57).

> Who shall separate us from the love of Christ?
> Shall tribulation, or distress, or persecution, or
> famine, or nakedness, or peril, or sword? As it is
> written: "For Your sake we are killed all day long;
> we are accounted as sheep for the slaughter."
> Yet in all these things we are more than conquerors
> through Him who loved us (Rom. 8:35-37).

A conqueror faces opposition and overcomes it, arising victorious in the midst of battles! Paul grabbed hold of this, and his anxiety was changed to hope. He wrote:

> Therefore I will boast all the more gladly about
> my weaknesses, so that Christ's power may rest
> on me. That is why, for Christ's sake, I delight in
> weaknesses, in insults, in hardships, in persecu-
> tions, in difficulties. For when I am weak, then I
> am strong (2 Cor. 12:9b-10, NIV).

Notice he says, "I delight in." How often do we see people delighting in reproaches, needs, persecutions and distresses? Only a person who is hidden in Christ (Gal. 2:20) can take pleasure in such things. This is one who lives to exalt Christ. Paul knew he could trust God's grace to sustain him until Christ was magnified.

Paul loved Jesus more than his own life. He was pre-pared to die — and was most willing to live — for Him. Look closely at his letter to the Philippians:

> According to my earnest expectation and hope
> that in nothing I shall be ashamed, but with all
> boldness, as always, so now also Christ will be
> magnified in my body, whether by life or by
> death (Phil. 1:20).

It didn't matter to Paul whether he would glorify Christ

in life or death. It only mattered that Christ was glorified. Paul was not referring to a death at the hands of sickness and disease. Jesus bore that for us on the cross. Sickness and disease don't bring Him glory. To believe we glorify Jesus by dying of disease is as erroneous as believing Jesus is glorified if we were to die in bondage to sin. He bore both on the cross (Is. 53:4-5). Psalm 103:2-3 says, "Bless the Lord, O my soul, and forget not all His benefits: who forgives all your iniquities, who heals all your diseases." As we can see, Paul is not talking about sickness or disease. Our attitude should be, Lord, however You will be glorified, have Your way, but the devil will not have his!

Paul's selfless love produced a boldness that no intimidation could penetrate. (Look again at Philippians 1:20!) Knowing he would face persecution and threats in every city, he pressed on. He feared no man. Paul shared with the elders of Ephesus:

> And see, now I go bound in the spirit to Jerusalem, not knowing the things that will happen to me there, except that the Holy Spirit testifies in every city, saying that chains and tribulations await me (Acts 20:22-23).

Wow — what a prophetic word! I wonder how many today would run to and fro for a word like this? No, they wouldn't want to hear this kind. We all like to hear good things, but God also warns of hardship in order to provide hope and courage. Paul strengthened new converts by telling them, "We must through many tribulations enter the kingdom of God" (Acts 14:22).

I wonder how we would respond if we received a prophetic word that persecutions and opposition await us at every turn. Of course, I am not saying that every time we get a genuine word from God it should be of this nature.

The problem is that a lot of the words that are given encourage the wrong things in the individuals seeking them. They are nice, comfortable words about how people will prosper in business or ministry, and all will be well for them. Often people end up seeking and serving God only for what He can do for them. Their love is not yet interested in magnifying Him, whether by life or death. Observe Paul's response to the prophetic word about chains and tribulations:

> But none of these things move me; nor do I count my life dear to myself, so that I may finish my race with joy, and the ministry which I received from the Lord Jesus, to testify to the gospel of the grace of God (Acts 20:24).

The key to Paul's boldness is that he did not consider his life dear. He also understood that God's plan for his life included facing trials and persecutions. His love for Jesus was greater than his love for life itself. Paul's life points to the secret of finishing the race. Lay down your life and take up Christ's. Often this will mean we lay down what is comfortable and pick up the uncomfortable — the cross.

Are You Sure This Gospel Is American?

I know this doesn't sound like our modern Western Christianity. It is quite different from what we have lived and preached in the 1980s and 1990s. I will be the first to admit I have fallen short. I have met up with "oil press" situations over the past ten years only to have my heart exposed. Like Peter I've grieved when I saw my empty promises and true heart condition. I've cried out to the Lord on numerous occasions, asking Him to change my heart. I have *learned* to be grateful for the strengthening of trials (1 Pet. 1:6-7). I have come to a clearer understanding of the following scripture:

> Therefore, since Christ suffered for us in the
> flesh, arm yourselves also with the same mind,
> for he who has suffered in the flesh has ceased
> from sin, that he no longer should live the rest
> of his time in the flesh for the lusts [desires] of
> men, but for the will of God (1 Pet. 4:1-2).

We are matured in the midst of suffering. I'm not talking
about the religious concept of suffering — accepting ill-
ness or poverty as if they earned you credit with God. Nor
am I referring to suffering because of ignorance and
unruly or ungodly behavior. God gets no glory out of that!
The sufferings we encounter will be those that Christ
experienced — tempted in all points yet without sin (Heb.
4:15). The suffering Peter describes is the resistance a person faces when his own flesh or those around him
pressure him to go one way while the will of God directs
him to go another. At this point intimidation can gain
advantage if we are not rooted in our love for Jesus.

Like Peter I want to follow Jesus to that place where I
will not merely *say* I will lose my physical life for Him,
but where I will accept the death of my own life and
desires. Let Him alone be glorified! This is accomplished
by His grace. He gives His grace to the humble (James
4:6). This is why Paul could say in the face of persecution, "I delight in." Look at what the apostle John said
about those who overcame Satan:

> And they overcame him by the blood of the Lamb
> and by the word of their testimony, and they did
> not love their lives to the death (Rev. 12:11).

I have heard this scripture quoted time and time again.
But only part of it. Most people stop too soon — they

leave off the last part. It is this portion that is unpopular in our Western culture. We will never win the battle over intimidation unless we refuse to love our lives even to the death. If we love our lives, we will seek to save them.

Men and women of God, now you know the truth: The only way to conquer intimidation is to lose your life. Cry out to God as you read. Don't draw back but dare to believe. Ask Him to fill your heart with this love — His love, the kind that never withdraws. Ask Him for His grace to overcome the obstacles you face. Ask Him to grant you the privilege of going into the hard places. Pray to be on the cutting edge of what He is doing in the earth. Don't ask for a life of ease. Instead ask for one that glorifies Him.

"But What About This Man?"

Let's go back to when Jesus cooked breakfast for His disciples after His resurrection. Jesus didn't give Peter a "blessing" prophecy after their breakfast. Yet Jesus' words held the promise that Peter would overcome his greatest fear, no longer fulfilling his own desires in his own strength. Jesus told him he would be martyred — losing his life because of his loyalty to Jesus. Peter would conquer what he could not face before. Jesus saw the new Peter, the one he would become. He saw the completed work.

Peter still was not ready. After hearing what would happen, he turned and saw John the apostle and asked Jesus, "But Lord, what about this man?" (John 21:21). Peter was still comparing himself to others. He was basically saying, "If I have to go through this, what does he have to do?"

Jesus answered, "If I will that he remain till I come, what is that to you? You follow Me" (v. 22).

In other words, it doesn't matter. Don't compare yourself with others. Just follow Me! So many people measure their lives and ministries by what others do and say. You

133

don't want to measure yourself by the wrong standard. There is a big difference between a centimeter and a kilometer. The majority of people in our churches live their lives as they please, in ease and comfort. When we compare ourselves to each other we look pretty good (and very lukewarm). It is a false comfort to say, "I'm as good as the crowd." The deception of this is believing that if you're OK, then I'm OK. However, we have one standard, one common unit of measure. We do not use as standards other preachers or churches, nor our brothers and sisters. Our standard is Jesus! He did not tell Peter to follow John. He said, "Follow Me!"

The path Jesus walked was a path of self-denial. Just wishing for or desiring to follow Jesus is not enough. We must do it! Read the following:

> When He had called the people to Himself, with His disciples also, He said to them, "Whoever desires to come after Me, let him deny himself, and take up his cross, and follow Me. For whoever desires to save his life will lose it" (Mark 8:34-35a).

Notice He said that all you have to do is desire to save your life and you will lose it! Wow! Desiring the things that this world pursues — even if you never attain them — will cost you your life. However, look carefully at what Jesus goes on to say:

> But whoever loses his life for My sake and the gospel's will save it (Mark 8:35b).

Notice He did not say, whoever *desires* to lose his life for My sake. Desiring is not enough! Peter desired to follow Jesus the night he betrayed Him. But his motivation was not backed by God's love or His power. Therefore, he was overcome.

Examine Your Heart

As you read, examine your motives. Are you a true disciple of Jesus Christ, or do you desire to follow Him only if it is within your parameters? Do you stay in your own boundaries, far from the border of self-sacrifice? Is it possible these boundaries will keep you from the paths Jesus walks and will eventually disqualify you (see 2 Cor. 13:5)?

To decide whether or not to follow Jesus, we must first know the cost. Yes, that is right. It will cost you. It requires nothing less than your entire life. Listen as Jesus outlines this to the multitudes who desired to follow Him:

> Now great multitudes went with Him. And He turned and said to them, "If anyone comes to Me and does not hate his father and mother, wife and children, brothers and sisters, yes, and his own life also, he cannot be My disciple.
>
> And whoever does not bear his cross and come after Me cannot be My disciple. For which of you, intending to build a tower, does not sit down first and count the cost, whether he has enough to finish it — lest, after he has laid the foundation, and is not able to finish, all who see it begin to mock him, saying, "This man began to build and was not able to finish."...So likewise, whoever of you does not forsake all that he has cannot be My disciple (Luke 14:25-30, 33).

This is what it costs to endure to the end. We have just read in the book of Revelation that those who overcome do not love their lives, even unto death. Unfortunately, that would not be an accurate description of the church in America today.

I could give many examples of Christian men and women who still own their lives. When I was pastoring, a young lady came to me complaining, "Pastor John, I have such a terrible self-image. Please pray for me to have a better self-image."

I looked at her and said, "That's your problem!"

She was baffled. She expected a long counseling session with prayer at the end. She was expecting me to be nice and sweet in order for her to feel better about herself. My reply shook her. But it is the truth that sets us free — not talking about our problems without dealing with their roots.

I questioned her, "Where do you find references to self-esteem or a good self-image in the Bible? Jesus said in order to follow Him you must die! Have you ever seen a dead person sit up in a casket and say, 'Hey! Why did you put me in this outfit? I don't like it! And why did you style my hair like this? What are people going to think?'"

I wanted to show her that self-esteem and a good self-image are not in the Bible. Feeling good about yourself is not a requirement for loving and following Jesus. Her focus was on the temporary, not the eternal.

We cannot serve God only when we feel good about ourselves, when we are excited or when everything is going our way. We would call people who behave this way "fair-weather friends." Now there are fair-weather Christians. They are unwise. Eventually they will have to face something that will not fit into their parameters. It could happen at any stage of their walk. If they are not prepared, they will quit. They may go to church, pay tithes and give offerings, speak with tongues and say the right things, but in their hearts they have given up their pursuit of God. The love of God knows no limit. If we are to walk with Him, we must remove our limits.

A Changed Man

When we look at Peter in the book of Acts, it is hard to believe he is the same man who cowered and denied

Christ before servants. After the infilling of the Holy Spirit he boldly and fearlessly proclaimed Jesus as Lord and Messiah throughout Jerusalem. He was arrested and brought before the leaders, the priests who had crucified Jesus. Now it was not before their servants that he stood, but before the very council that condemned Jesus. He looked at them and with great boldness declared, "You were the ones who crucified Jesus Christ the Messiah, and there is no salvation in any other than Him" (see Acts 4:8-12).

The boldness of Peter and John caused the council to be amazed, and they could say nothing against the work God had done. These men were masters at control, so they resorted to intimidation.

They said among themselves, "But so that it spreads no further among the people, let us severely threaten them, that from now on they speak to no man in this name" (Acts 4:17).

Remember, these leaders had just crucified Jesus. And Jesus had already told Peter that he would die as Jesus had. These were not idle threats. Yet, even in the face of possible death, Peter and John boldly stated, "Whether it is right in the sight of God to listen to you more than to God, you judge. For we cannot but speak the things which we have seen and heard" (Acts 4:19-20).

Except for John, Peter was alone before the council. There was no one to impress or back him up. But now he had a different kind of boldness. It was fueled by his love for Jesus. He and John were released and rejoined the disciples, reporting what had happened and the threats that were made. Now watch what these men ask God to do:

> Now, Lord, look on their threats, and grant to Your servants that with all boldness they may speak Your word, by stretching out Your hand to heal, and that signs and wonders may be done through the name of Your holy Servant Jesus (Acts 4:29-30).

These men asked God for more of the very thing that got them into trouble. They knew that preaching the gospel would put their lives at risk. But they continued to preach, and God was faithful to perform with great miracles. They did not allow the gift of God to become dormant because of intimidation. In fact the power of God was so strong that the sick were brought out into the streets of Jerusalem, and they were healed when the shadow of Peter fell on them (Acts 5:15).

The high priest and the council made good on their threats. They had the disciples arrested and put in jail. The high priest said, "Did we not strictly command you not to teach in this name? And look, you have filled Jerusalem with your doctrine" (Acts 5:28).

Again, Peter responded boldly:

> We ought to obey God rather than men. The God of our fathers raised up Jesus whom you murdered by hanging on a tree. Him God has exalted to His right hand to be Prince and Savior, to give repentance to Israel and forgiveness of sins. And we are His witnesses to these things, and so also is the Holy Spirit whom God has given to those who obey Him (Acts 5:29-32).

What courage and boldness! The disciples would not be intimidated. Peter no longer sought to preserve his life. He was free from selfishness and filled with God's Holy Spirit. God's love abounded in his heart. Just as Romans 5:5 says, "The love of God has been poured out in our hearts by the Holy Spirit who was given to us."

It's clear that the Holy Spirit brings God's love into our lives. But it's also clear from Peter that the Holy Spirit is given to those who *obey*. Too many Christians want the love without the obedience.

Speaking in tongues does not guarantee that the love of

God abides in your heart. The infilling of the Holy Spirit is not a one-time experience. It doesn't matter how well you know the Scriptures and how well you speak in tongues. If you are not living an obedient life before God, your love will grow cold. With every disobedience, that love can diminish!

Jesus said a sign of the last days would be the love of God growing cold in the hearts of Christians because of lawlessness or disobedience (Matt. 24:12). The love Jesus refers to is *agape*. Only those who have received Jesus possess this love. It is possible to be filled but lack the genuine love of the Spirit!

Peter and John's obedience bought them great boldness and filled their hearts with love.

> And when they had called for the apostles and beaten them, they commanded that they should not speak in the name of Jesus, and let them go. So they departed from the presence of the council, rejoicing that they were counted worthy to suffer shame for His name (Acts 5:40-41).

Peter and John were not intimidated by the leaders; in fact, they were full of joy. These are two very different disciples from the ones asleep in the garden. They rejoiced to be counted worthy and given another chance to show their love and faithfulness. Peter now not only loves affectionately, but also with his whole being.

Foxe's Christian Martyrs of the World records that Peter was martyred, just as Jesus said. When he was about to be crucified, Peter is reported to have said, "I am not worthy to die in the manner that my Lord did." So they hung him on the cross upside down! Peter left this world a conqueror. Hallelujah!

*You will serve
who you fear.*

Chapter 11

FEAR OF GOD
VS. FEAR OF MAN

All we've read and studied now leads up to this most crucial element in dealing with intimidation. It is not only important when facing intimidation, but also in every area of life! I'm talking about the fear of the Lord.

The church does not understand the fear of the Lord. This is unfortunate because it is a significant element to a triumphant Christian life. Isaiah prophesied concerning Jesus, "His delight is in the fear of the Lord" (Is. 11:3). His delight should be ours!

The man who fears God will be led in God's ways (Ps. 25:12). That man "shall dwell in prosperity, and his descendants shall inherit the earth" (v. 13).

We are told the fear of the Lord is the beginning of

141

wisdom and the beginning of knowledge of Him (Prov. 9:10; 1:7; 2:5). It will prolong our days (Prov. 10:27). We are warned that no one will see the Lord without holiness which is perfected by the fear of the Lord (Heb. 12:14; 2 Cor. 7:1). And this is just a sampling of what the Bible says about the fear of the Lord.

The only way to walk totally free from intimidation is to walk in the fear of the Lord. The Bible says, "In the fear of the Lord there is strong confidence" (Prov. 14:26). Strong confidence produces the boldness we need to go God's way rather than man's way. Let's examine the differences between the fear of God and the fear of man.

Defining the Fear of God and the Fear of Man

First, what is the fear of God? It includes, but is more than, respecting Him. Fearing Him means to give Him the place of glory, honor, reverence, thanksgiving, praise and preeminence He deserves. (Notice it is what *He* deserves, not what we *think* He deserves). He holds this position in our lives when we esteem Him and His desires over and above our own. We will hate what He hates and love what He loves, trembling in His presence and at His word.

Second, let's examine the fear of man. To fear man is to stand in alarm, anxiety, awe, dread and suspicion, cowering before mortal men. When entrapped by this fear we will live on the run, hiding from harm or reproach, and constantly avoiding rejection and confrontation. We become so busy safeguarding ourselves and serving men we are ineffective in our service for God. Afraid of what man can do to us, we will not give God what He deserves.

The Bible tells us, "The fear of man brings a snare" (Prov. 29:18). A snare is a trap. Fearing man steals your God-given authority. His gift then lies dormant in you. You feel powerless to do what is right because the empowering of God is inactive.

Isaiah 51:7-13 admonishes, "Listen to Me, you who know righteousness, you people in whose heart is My law: Do not fear the reproach of men, nor be afraid of their insults...Who are you that you should be afraid of a man who will die, and the son of a man who will be made like grass? And you forget the Lord your Maker."

When we please men to escape reproach, we forget the Lord. We depart from His service. "For if I still pleased men, I would not be a bondservant of Christ" (Gal. 1:10).

You will serve and obey whom you fear! If you fear man, you will serve him. If you fear God, you will serve Him. You cannot fear God if you fear man because you cannot serve two masters (Matt. 6:24)! On the other hand, you will not be afraid of man if you fear God!

Should New Testament Believers Fear God?

The fear of the Lord is not a dead, Old Testament doctrine. It is a way of life. If you love God, you will fear Him alone. Your fear of God will swallow up all lesser fears.

I am grieved when I hear people speak of God as if He were their errand boy. A person who speaks of Him in this manner does not truly know the Lord. Even Jesus' closest disciples called Him Lord and Master (John 20:28). When we treat the Lord as familiar, we lose perspective of His proper place.

This type of attitude will cause us to behave irreverently. We see evidence of this both in church and in the private lives of "believers." They call themselves believers, but does their lifestyle show it? Often I am grieved as I watch the way people act in church. Before service they run each other over to get a seat or become upset if someone else is in theirs. They talk and carry on during service. Then they get up and leave if they think the service is too long or if they don't like what they hear.

It is alarming to see their apparent lack of respect for

their pastors. They talk about God's servants as the news media talks about politicians. Perhaps a lot of ministers have acted more like politicians than men of God. But they are still God's servants, and His to judge. When we fear God we will respect the things of His house and the servants He appoints. David did not raise his hand against God's anointed, King Saul, even after Saul killed eighty-five priests of the Lord (1 Sam. 22:11-23). David feared God!

I am grieved by what many believers listen to, watch and read. In some homes I've wondered if there were any difference between the way they lived and the world lived. In their pursuit to be balanced, normal and accepted, they have forgotten God does not call "normal" what the world calls "normal." When you truly love God and fear Him alone, you will live a life of consecration, not worldliness. Peter exhorted:

> But as He who called you is holy, you also be holy in all your conduct, because it is written, "Be holy, for I am holy." And if you call on the Father, who without partiality judges according to each one's work, conduct yourselves throughout the time of your stay here in fear (1 Pet. 1:15-17).

The fear of God is a great motivation for keeping us from ungodliness.

Is the Church Afraid?

In Acts 2 the disciples were filled with the Holy Spirit and spoke with tongues and prophesied. They were so filled that they acted like drunken men. Laughter and joy overflowed in these new believers. God was strengthening and refreshing them. God delights in doing this. He is not a vindictive God who delights in gloom, but rather He delights in love, mercy, righteousness, peace and joy.

The disciples saw many people saved over the next few days. But some of these new converts had come to the Lord for blessings rather than for who He is. This caused them not to give God the reverence He deserved. They gradually grew too "familiar" with the Lord. This familiarity caused them to treat the things of God as if they were common. They did not tremble at His presence or word. We see evidence of this in Acts chapter 5.

A man and his wife brought an offering from a plot of land they sold. It was not the whole amount they received from the sale. But, they wanted it to appear that way so they would look good in the sight of the other believers. They honored appearance over truth and feared man over God. They brought the offering, lied (most would consider this just a white one) — and fell over dead.

They died because they lied in the presence of God's glory. I used to think, as I'm sure you have, There have been people who have done the same in the presence of preachers today and not fallen over dead. Why?

I believe it is because the presence of God was more powerful at the time of the book of Acts than it is today. For example, Acts records that after that incident that Peter walked the streets of Jerusalem and the sick were healed as his shadow touched them (Acts 5:15). We don't see those kinds of miracles today.

I believe that as His presence and glory increases, there will be similar accounts to the one in Acts chapter 5. Notice what happened after they fell over dead.

> So great fear came upon all the church and upon all who heard these things (Acts 5:11).

The deep awe and reverence for the Lord was restored. They realized they needed to rethink their treatment of God's presence and anointing. Remember, God has said:

By those who come near Me I must be regarded as holy; and before all the people I must be glorified (Lev. 10:3).

When God Is Quiet, Our Hearts Are Revealed

God has withheld His glory to test and prepare us. Will we be reverent even when His presence is not manifest? In so many ways the modern church has behaved like the children of Israel. In fact, Paul said their experiences were written down as examples for us (1 Cor. 10:6).

The Israelites were excited when God blessed them, and performed miracles for them. When God parted the Red Sea, brought them across on dry ground and then buried their enemies, they sang, danced and shouted for victory (Ex. 15:1-21). However, a few days later when His mighty power was not apparent, and food and drink were scarce, they complained against God (Ex. 15:22).

Later, Moses brought the people to Mount Sinai to consecrate them to God. God came down on the mountain in the sight of all His people. It was quite awesome, with thunder and lightning and a thick cloud on the mountain. Moses then brought the people out of the camp to meet God, but "when the people saw it, they trembled and stood afar off" (Ex. 20:10-18). They pulled back in terror — not in the fear of God, but in the fear for their own lives. When God came down they realized they loved their own lives more than they loved God.

They told Moses, "'You speak with us, and we will hear; but let not God speak with us, lest we die.' And Moses said to the people, 'Do not fear; for God has come to test you, and that His fear may be before you, so that you may not sin.'" (Ex. 20:19-20).

Notice that the fear of God gives you power over sin. Proverbs 16:6 says, "By the fear of the Lord one departs from evil."

Exodus 20:21 continues the account, "So the people stood afar off, but Moses drew near the thick darkness where God was." Moses told God what they had said and how they were afraid. God answered, "They are right in all that they have spoken. Oh that they had such a heart in them that they would fear Me and always keep all My commandments, that it might be well with them and with their children forever!" (Deut. 5:28-29).

Notice the people drew back while Moses drew near. This reveals the difference between Moses and Israel. Moses feared God; therefore, he was unafraid. The people did not fear God; therefore, they were afraid. The fear of God draws you toward God's presence, not away from it. However, the fear of man causes you to withdraw from God and His glory.

When we are bound by the fear of man we will feel more comfortable in the presence of men than in the presence of God, even in church! The reason: the presence of God lays open our hearts and brings conviction.

Not Sinai but Zion

To prove that the fear of God is a New Testament reality we go to this account in the book of Hebrews:

> For you have not come to the mountain that may be touched and that burned with fire, and to blackness and darkness and tempest, and the sound of a trumpet and the voice of words, so that those who heard it begged that the word should not be spoken to them anymore. But you have come to Mount Zion (Heb. 12:18-22).

First we are reminded of what happened on Sinai. Then we are told about the mountain we have come to, called Zion. God spoke on the earth from that mountain at Sinai.

Now the same God speaks from heaven on this new mountain, Zion.

> See that you do not refuse Him who speaks. For if they did not escape who refused Him who spoke on earth, much more shall we not escape if we turn away from Him who speaks from heaven (Heb. 12:25).

Notice the words, "much more"! Our judgment is much more severe when we don't listen to and obey the voice of God. The grace we are given under the New Testament is not for us to use to live as we please. Why didn't the Israelites heed His voice? They did not fear God. Keep this in mind as you continue to read and you will see clearly that the reason people do not listen under the new covenant is the same:

> Therefore, since we are receiving a kingdom which cannot be shaken, let us have grace, by which we may serve God acceptably with reverence and godly fear. For our God is a consuming fire (Heb. 12:28).

Notice it says "reverence and godly fear." If the fear of God were limited to just reverence, the writer would not have separated the concept of godly fear from it. Also notice that the writer did not conclude with, "For our God is a God of love," but rather, "Our God is a consuming fire." This statement about God corresponds with the reason the children of Israel backed away from His presence. "For this great fire will consume us; if we hear the voice of the Lord our God anymore, then we shall die" (Deut. 5:25). God has not changed! He is still holy, still the consuming fire!

Yes, He is love, but He is also a consuming fire. In our churches we have emphasized God's love and heard very little on the fear of God. Because we have not preached the whole counsel of God, our view of love is warped.

The love we've preached is a weak love. It does not have the power to lead us into consecrated living. It has dampened our fire and left us lukewarm. We have become like spoiled children who do not reverence their father! If we do not grow in the fear of the Lord, we risk the danger of becoming familiar with God and treating as common the things He considers holy.

Note this verse also: "Let us have grace, by which we may serve God acceptably with reverence and godly fear" (Heb. 12:28). Grace is not given merely to cover up our irreverence and sin; it is given to empower us .to serve God acceptably. And the acceptable way of serving him is out of love with reverence and godly fear.

Along these lines Paul also wrote: "Work out your own salvation with fear and trembling" (Phil. 2:12). Where is our fear and trembling? Have we forgotten He is the just *Judge?* Have we forgotten His judgment? Read the following exhortation carefully.

> Do not be haughty, but fear. For if God did not spare the natural branches [Israel], He may not spare you either. Therefore consider the goodness and severity of God: on those who fell, severity; but toward you, goodness, if you continue in His goodness. Otherwise you also will be cut off (Rom. 11:20b-22).

We have become experts in His goodness; however, it is not just His goodness we are to consider. We must understand the severity of God as well. His goodness draws us to His heart, and His severity keeps us from pride and all manner of sin. A person who only considers the goodness forsakes the fear that will keep him from pride and worldliness. Likewise, the person who only considers the severity of God is easily ensnared in legalism. It is both the love and the fear of God that keep us on the narrow path to life.

I hope you realize I am purposefully emphasizing this fear of God that has been so neglected in our modern church. I dearly love God and take great joy in being His child and in the privilege of serving Him. I know that it is the goodness of God that leads us to repentance (Rom. 2:4). I also know it is the fear of God and His judgment which keeps us from sinning willfully.

> For if we sin willfully after we have received the knowledge of the truth, there no longer remains a sacrifice for sins, but a certain fearful expectation of judgment, and fiery indignation which will devour the adversaries. Anyone who has rejected Moses' law dies without mercy on the testimony of two or three witnesses.
>
> Of how much worse punishment, do you suppose, will he be thought worthy who has trampled the Son of God underfoot, counted the blood of the covenant by which he was sanctified a common thing, and insulted the Spirit of grace? For we know Him who said, "Vengeance is Mine, I will repay," says the Lord. And again, "The Lord will judge His people." It is a fearful thing to fall into the hands of the living God (Heb. 10:26-31).

A person is seduced into sin when he counts as common or familiar what God esteems as holy. Too often we take lightly the things God takes seriously, and we treat seriously the things God treats lightly. We are very serious about appearing respectable to other people, but that's not as important to God as the motives of our hearts.

I've known men who were entrapped in sin, all the while saying, "I love Jesus." They measured their spiritual condition by what they felt for Jesus. But did they love Him enough to die to the sin that bound them? No, they had no fear of God!

As I visited one minister in prison who had fallen into sexual immorality and financial corruption, he told me, "John, I always loved Jesus, even when I was deceived. He was my Savior but not my Master." He had made decisions motivated by the fear of man. He wanted to please people. He desired the accolades that come from men. This led him into corruption. In that prison God showed him His love and mercy, and taught Him the fear of the Lord. He now fears the Lord and has been restored.

Refusing God's Invitation

Returning to the illustration of Mount Sinai, I want to point out something most people miss. God instructed both Moses and Aaron to come up to the mountain (Ex. 19:24). Moses went up, but for some reason we find Aaron back in the camp! (Ex. 32:1) I believe Aaron returned to camp because he was more comfortable in the presence of the other "believers" than in the presence of God. Are we not like this in our churches today? We are more comfortable going to church, fellowshipping with other Christians and keeping busy with ministry duties than with the Lord. We avoid being alone in His presence, instead surrounding ourselves with people and activity, hoping this will hide our emptiness.

Joshua, on the other hand, had a heart after God. He wanted to be as close to the presence of God as possible. He stayed at the foot of the mountain for forty days while Moses was with God (Ex. 32:17). He got as close as he could without going where only Moses and Aaron had been invited. Joshua feared God enough not to be presumptuous.

As Joshua waited at the mountain, the people in the camp grew restless. They were in a strange land; their leader had been gone for more than a month; and God still had not revealed Himself. They started questioning God and Moses.

> The people gathered together to Aaron, and said to him, "Come, make us gods that shall go before us; for as for this Moses, the man who brought us up out of the land of Egypt, we do not know what has become of him (Ex. 32:1).

In appearance, they respected and feared God. "Oh, Moses," they had pleaded, "He is too awesome for us. You go talk to Him and tell us what He says. We'll listen and obey." They had just seen how terrible and powerful God was, yet they did not fear Him as they built idols for themselves. Now that God was quiet, their true nature was revealed.

We can easily fear God while He is doing miracles and demonstrating of His power. But God is looking for those who will also reverence and fear Him when they do not perceive His presence or power, like children who obey even when their father is not watching. The truly obedient are so when no one is around to monitor them!

God said to Israel, "Is it not because I have held My peace from of old that you do not fear Me?" (Is. 57:11). He essentially asked, "Why don't My people fear Me?" Then He answered His own question by observing that the people did not fear Him because He had not manifested Himself in terrifying power for some time. In other words, when the people didn't see Him displayed awesomely, they acted as if He weren't there. God's silence exposed the people's true heart motive.

It is in the midst of the desert, while facing trials, not in an anointed powerful service, that a true believer is revealed. What a person is like in the "press" is what he is really like. Watch what Aaron did under pressure:

> And Aaron said to them, "Break off the golden earrings which are in the ears of your wives, your sons, and your daughters, and bring them to me." So all the people broke off the golden earrings which were in their ears, and brought them to Aaron. And he received the gold from their hand, and he fashioned it with an engraving tool, and made a molded calf. Then they said, "This is your god, O Israel, that brought you out of the land of Egypt!" (Ex. 32:2-4).

They made an idol out of God's blessing, the spoils of Egypt. But even more alarming is that Aaron, the one who would not come up the mountain, made the idol. He had been Moses' spokesman. He had stood at his side and watched every great miracle and plague. But now he feared the people and gave them what they wanted. He feared man more than God so he was easily intimidated by the people. There was no boldness in him, the gift of God was dormant. This made him a weak leader. When confronted by Moses, he blamed the people who had intimidated him.

> Aaron said, "Do not let the anger of my lord become hot. You know the people, that they are set on evil. For they said to me, "Make us gods that shall go before us; as for this Moses, the man who brought us out of the land of Egypt, we do not know what has become of him." And I said to them, "Whoever has any gold, let them break it off." So they gave it to me, and I cast it into the fire, and this calf came out (Ex. 32:22-24).

Aaron did not take responsibility for what he had done. Yes, his assessment of the people was correct. It was their idea, not Aaron's. But because he feared them he was not strong enough to break the intimidation of the crowd and lead them correctly. He was entrapped by the fear of man.

Leaders who fear men will back down and give the people what they want rather than what they need! They become easy prey for intimidation. It doesn't matter how much the leader says he loves God and His people, as long as he fears man he will never see true progress in himself or the people he leads!

The man who fears God is only concerned with what God says about him. The man who fears men is more concerned with what men think about him than God. He offends God in order not to offend man.

I have watched leaders make decisions to give the people what they wanted. Their motives were to keep their popularity with the people. Of course, they would never admit this and were possibly not even aware of it. They justified their decisions, reasoning, "We don't want to offend people," or "This is the best for all concerned," or "More people can be ministered to if we do this," and so on. The kingdom of God is not a democracy. It is a kingdom. Popularity is not important. They did not realize they were motivated by fear and intimidation. Their actions were not rooted in a love for the people but in love for themselves.

What Happens When We Don't Fear God?

God said to Moses, "Oh, that they had such a heart in them that they would fear Me" (Deut. 5:29). But the people did not, and look what happened.

After a year of living in the wilderness it was time to go and take the promised land. The Lord told Moses, "Send men to spy out the land of Canaan which I am giving to the children of Israel" (Num. 13:1). Notice He said, "I am *giving...*" He did not say, "Spy out the land and see if they can take it."

So Moses sent them. They spied for forty days, and they discovered the inhabitants were well-established in this land, and the cities were very large and well-guarded.

All twelve spies saw the same people, the same armies, the same large fortified cities and the same giants. Joshua and Caleb were ready to go in at once and take what God had promised. However, the other ten spies were intimidated by what they saw. They saw only big armies and giants, whereas Joshua and Caleb saw how good and faithful God was!

The ten spies told the people it would be impossible to take the land. They had been slaves for more than four hundred years and were not skilled in war like the armies they saw were. The people immediately became afraid and started complaining.

> Why has the Lord brought us to this land to fall
> by the sword, that our wives and children
> should become victims? Would it not be better
> for us to return to Egypt? (Num. 14:3).

In this verse we find the root of man's fear: Would it not be better for us? These people were intimidated because they thought only of themselves. They did not say, "What God says is best." Instead they asked, "What is best for us?"

How clear can it be? The root of the fear of man is the love of self. When you love your life, you seek to save it. You will be intimidated by anything that threatens it.

God brought these people to the place where they had no choice but to trust Him. It appeared they would all be destroyed by the inhabitants of this new land. But instead of trusting God, they acted as if God had saved them from the Egyptians only to have the Canaanites kill them. Of course this sounds ridiculous, but we all may face times when we are required to follow the Lord into situations that appear dangerous or damaging to our lives.

We can only follow Him in these circumstances when we have settled in our hearts that God is good. There is only good in Him. He would never do anything to us for only His benefit at our eternal expense or harm! We must remember, God judges everything by eternity, while man judges by seventy or eighty years!

God's Rejection or Man's?

Caleb and Joshua chose the difficult road. God said they had a different spirit in them and had followed Him fully. All the rest did not want their welfare jeopardized by obeying God. God was faithful to Caleb and Joshua. They were the only ones of that generation to enter the promised land (see Num. 14:24,30).

Those who sought to save their lives forfeited them. God pronounced their fate by saying, "But as for you, your carcasses shall fall in this wilderness...and you shall know My rejection" (Num. 14:32,34). It is a sobering thought to know that many will be rejected by God because they feared rejection by man.

I pray that we all will learn to delight ourselves in the fear of the Lord. For "the fear of the Lord is a fountain of life, to turn one away from the snares of death" (Prov. 14:27). In the next chapter you'll see how the fear of the Lord will help you walk in God's will during times of intimidation.

*The fear of the Lord
produces
confidence and boldness.*

Chapter 12

ACT OR REACT?

Intimidation can come via circumstances, thoughts or people. Most people struggle with intimidation that comes through other people. The fear of man is an accurate description of this type of pressure.

The fear of man causes us to avoid rejection, harm and reproach from man without considering God's rejection. A person who fears man will offend the One he cannot see in order not to offend the one he can.

Jesus exhorted us, "My friends, do not be afraid of those who kill the body, and after that have no more that they can do. But I will show you whom you should fear: Fear Him who, after He has killed, has the power to cast into hell; yes, I say to you, fear Him!" (Luke 12:4-5).

If you fear men, when God leads you into difficulty or

hardship, you will try to protect and preserve yourself. Instead of seeking God's will, you seek to exercise your own. However, if you fear the Lord, you can walk through any difficulty in a manner that honors God. You recognize that He alone can keep you, and you will trust that He knows what is best in the eternal scheme of things.

There's a powerful promise in Proverbs about the fear of the Lord:

> Ir. the fear of the Lord there is strong confidence, and His children will have a place of refuge. The fear of the Lord is a fountain of life, to turn one away from the snares of death (Prov. 14:26-27).

On the other hand, Scripture says clearly:

> The fear of man brings a snare (Prov. 29:25).

Intimidation is a snare or trap, but the fear of the Lord produces confidence and boldness, the exact tools it takes to free us from this trap of intimidation.

Pressure Reveals

I will contrast two kings. Both ruled the same kingdom; both bowed before the same God. One was rejected by God, and one esteemed by God as a man after His own heart. By contrasting these lives we find a great clarity and understanding of the differences between the fear of God and the fear of man. Let's look at one of the most dramatic and least studied incidents in the life of Saul. Here's the scene:

Saul had been reigning for two years. As with most positions, this "honeymoon" period did not reveal his true character. But with the passage of time his motives were exposed.

While Saul was at Michmash with his finest warriors, the Philistines gathered together to fight against him (1 Sam. 13:5-15). This was the strongest army Saul had faced. The enemy had thirty thousand chariots and six thousand horsemen, and the multitude of soldiers was compared to "the sand which is on the seashore." Needless to say, it was a huge army! Facing thirty thousand chariots is like facing thirty thousand tanks — plus, the army was so big it could not be counted! This was a very intimidating sight for the army of Israel.

In terror, Saul's soldiers hid themselves in thickets, holes, pits and behind rocks. They were overwhelmed. Some fled on foot, crossing the Jordan to the land of Gad and Gilead, while those who remained followed Saul, trembling with fear.

Before battles, Israel would make supplication before the Lord. Samuel had given a command from the Lord to Saul, telling him that he would be there at a set time to present the burnt offering to the Lord. Saul "waited seven days, according to the time set by Samuel. But Samuel did not come to Gilgal; and the people were scattered from him [Saul]" (1 Sam. 13:8).

Under pressure, Saul said, "Bring a burnt offering and peace offerings here to me." He offered the burnt offering, and as soon as he did, Samuel arrived.

Samuel asked Saul what he had done. Look carefully at Saul's reply:

> When I saw that the people were scattered from me, and that you did not come within the days appointed, and that the Philistines gathered together at Michmash, then I said, "The Philistines will now come down on me at Gilgal,

and I have not made supplication to the Lord."
Therefore I felt compelled, and offered a burnt
offering (1 Sam. 13:11-12).

Samuel then rebuked Saul by telling him that he had
done foolishly by not keeping the commandment of the
Lord.

Now that we've reviewed what happened, imagine
yourself in Saul's position. You are the leader. You and
your men have faced a massive army for more than seven
days. You are already greatly outnumbered, and each day
the enemy's ranks grow bigger as your army diminishes.
Your men are afraid of the enemy and go AWOL. And the
few that are left are shaking in terror. You're waiting on
God's prophet, and he doesn't show up on time to offer
the sacrifice!

There is tremendous pressure on you. This is an "oil press"
situation. Those around you urge you, "Do something, or we
will all die!" Will you wait as the Lord commanded, or will
you make a move to save yourself?

This was the situation that faced King Saul (see 1 Sam.
13:1-8). Unfortunately, he broke under pressure. In disobedience, he offered the sacrifices himself. Look at Saul's
excuses: "The Philistines [were coming] down on me...I
felt compelled" (1 Sam. 13:12). He made the sacrifices to
make himself look good to the people, and then he tried
to look spiritual with Samuel by saying, "I felt compelled."
In reality, he reacted and fell into intimidation's trap.

Do Something!

Most people at one time or another face this type of situation. Have you ever thought, I know God is telling me
to stand still, but I have to make a move in order to
change this situation I'm in.

I've been in situations when friends and those under

my authority have pleaded with me, "John, you have to do something!" Yet in my heart I knew God was not saying the same thing. He was silent.

One of the hardest things to do is to wait on God, especially when He is not saying anything! This is particularly true now. With our vast resources and money in America, we can usually make something happen even if God is not moving. We can create something that appears to be from God with the strength of our natural talents and abilities — and without God's involvement.

When it comes to making decisions, we often cannot find a chapter and verse that tells us what to do. We must know what God is saying to us at every moment. But when God does not seem to be speaking, He really is! He is saying, "Keep doing exactly what I told you to do. Nothing has changed!" This becomes especially difficult when we are under intimidation.

I want to share a word the Lord gave me one New Year's Day. I was overseas, sound asleep, exhausted from the forty-six-hour trip and a twice-a-day ministry schedule. Suddenly I awoke from my deep sleep at two o'clock in the morning. I knew that only the Lord could have awakened me this way, because I was strangely alert after having only three hours of sleep.

The Lord gave me a word that normally I would not share because it was personal. But I believe the Lord would have me share this in order to illustrate this point. I believe it will strengthen many of you who are in similar situations. Here is a portion of it:

> You have not felt focused; this has been a part of your testing. I have not allowed you to focus, to test you to see if you would move without My direction. Your not moving during My silence has pleased Me well. Because you did not move

163

when I did not say to, and because you didn't make your own plans, hoping that they were Mine, now you shall see great focus come. For I will give you and your wife great and specific plans that will bring you both great joy.

The Lord spoke to me at a time when my wife and I were both feeling stagnant. We had personal desires and needs that we felt were not being fulfilled. We both had been living under an extreme amount of pressure for a number of years. Friends who genuinely cared for us counseled us to make some moves, but we did not sense it was the word of the Lord. They were not wrong in telling us these things. They were only responding to the situation they saw us in. This was our test.

There were changes we could make to alleviate the pressure we were under. We would fight our doubts but wonder, Are we missing God? Yet deep in our hearts we both knew God had not instructed us to make any moves.

Before the first month of that new year was over we watched God do things beyond our wildest expectations! I don't know if I'd ever seen so much happen in just one month. It seemed God did more in that month than in the five years previous!

It is crucial that we do not react under pressure. We must act according to the word of the Lord.

A Man After the Heart of God

Saul was intimidated. His reputation, life and kingdom were at stake, so he moved when God commanded him to wait. After Samuel rebuked Saul, he pronounced this judgment on him:

But now your kingdom shall not continue. The Lord has sought for Himself a man after His own heart, and the Lord has commanded him to be commander over His people, because you have not kept what the Lord commanded you (1 Sam. 13:14).

Saul did not bow to intimidation in one incident only. Saul built a history of disobeying the Lord in high-pressure situations. In another incident he yielded to the desire of the people to take spoils from a town God had told them to destroy utterly. He did not want to lose the favor of the people. When confronted by Samuel, Saul admitted, "I have sinned, for I have transgressed the commandment of the Lord and your words, because I feared the people and obeyed their voice" (1 Sam. 15:24).

His next statement shows he was more concerned about his reputation than his disobedience. His words to Samuel betray his heart: "I have sinned; yet honor me now, please, before the elders of my people and before Israel" (1 Sam. 15:30).

Repeatedly Saul transgressed because he feared man. As he became more afraid, he became more of a dominating leader. This often happens with leaders who are insecure. They treat people harshly to make it seem as if they are in control, when actually they are covering up their own intimidation and fear.

Samuel told Saul that God would give the kingdom to a man who would keep His commands (1 Sam. 13:14). David was that man. I have heard some people say they have a heart after God, but I want to hear God say, as He said of David, "You have a heart after Me." I know this is a desire of every believer who loves Him! I have carefully studied David's life, desiring to know what it was about him that would cause the Lord to align Himself with David.

I noticed that David was careful not to do anything

without hearing the word of God on the matter. Over and over again in high-pressure situations he inquired for God's counsel (1 Sam. 20–31). Let's look at one extremely harrowing situation.

Can It Get Any Worse?

During the last year of Saul's reign, David and his men took refuge in the land of the Philistines. In a strange twist of fate, David and his men went to assemble with the Philistines when the Philistine army gathered against the Israelites. However, the Philistine lords were displeased when they saw the Hebrew men going to war with them. So they denied David and his men permission to fight with them.

The next morning David's troop left to return to their wives and children, who were in the city of Ziklag. The trip to the battlefield had been a failure, and David and his men must have felt unwanted. They were rejected not only by their own king and country, but also by the nation in which they took refuge. David could have felt quite alone — a man without a country. It was not a pleasant day. But this was nothing compared with what he was about to face. Read carefully what happened when he returned to his family, and allow yourself to imagine how he felt.

> Now it happened, when David and his men came to Ziklag, on the third day, that the Amalekites had invaded the South and Ziklag, attacked Ziklag and burned it with fire, and had taken captive the women and those who were there, from small to great; they did not kill anyone, but carried them away and went their way.
>
> So David and his men came to the city, and there it was, burned with fire; and their wives,

their sons, and their daughters had been taken captive. Then David and the people who were with him lifted up their voices and wept, until they had no more power to weep. And David's two wives, Ahinoam the Jezreelitess, and Abigail the widow of Nabal the Carmelite, had been taken captive (1 Sam. 30:1-5).

Can you imagine the pain he felt? His family had been kidnapped, everything dear had been stolen, and what was left, burned! Not only did he have his own family to be concerned about, but also the families of all his men. They had been feeling useless and without a country. Then they had returned to find their homes smoking and all that they loved gone. As if this weren't bad enough, look at what happened next:

Now David was greatly distressed, for the people spoke of stoning him, because the soul of all the people was grieved, every man for his sons and his daughters (1 Sam. 30:6).

Now the only ones left, the men who went to battle with him, were ready to stone him for leaving their wives and children unguarded! It could not get worse. This was even more difficult than what Saul faced. David had no human being to turn to. At least Saul still had a trembling army and family, and his own were not threatening to stone him.

Most believers hit a point in their lives when they feel all alone. I believe God allows this to happen. He does not cause it, for He is not the author of evil. But He will refrain from intervening because He has a purpose in these times of despair. David could have given up, started to pursue the enemy or found another way to appease his men. But look at what he did instead.

> But David strengthened himself in the Lord his God. Then David said to Abiathar the priest, Ahimelech's son, "Please bring the ephod here to me." And Abiathar brought the ephod to David. So David inquired of the Lord, saying, "Shall I pursue this troop? Shall I overtake them?" And He answered him, "Pursue, for you shall surely overtake them and without fail recover all" (1 Sam. 30:6-8).

Even under tremendous pressure, David would not move until he first received the counsel of the Lord. He strengthened himself by turning to the Lord. He reminded himself of God's faithfulness and covenant. Then he inquired what he should do. God said, "Pursue."

David did pursue. "So David recovered all that the Amalekites had carried away, and David rescued his two wives. And nothing of theirs was lacking, either small or great, sons or daughters, spoil or anything which they had taken from them; David recovered all" (1 Sam. 30:18-19).

What had appeared hopeless turned into a great victory! Nothing is too difficult for our God. David feared God more than he feared his men. This alone gave him confidence to turn to God first. This was quite different from Saul's reaction to pressure.

David *acted,* while Saul *reacted.* David could act and not react because he knew what God was saying. When we have the mind of Christ, we are equipped with the courage to act and not react.

A Sound Mind

In an earlier chapter we discovered that it takes boldness to break intimidation — not natural boldness, but boldness fueled by the godly virtues of power, love and a sound mind. This was our key verse:

Therefore I remind you to stir up the gift of God which is in you through the laying on of my hands. For God has not given us a spirit of fear, but of power and of love and of a sound mind (2 Tim. 1:6-7).

Let's look at how these three things produced the boldness in David that it took to withstand any intimidation he faced.

1. Power. He knew God, and he knew that God was greater and more powerful than anything David would face.

2. Love. He loved God more than himself.

3. A sound mind. He would not be moved until he had the word or mind of the Lord, no matter how great the pressure.

When our spirits are filled with power, love and the word of the Lord, we will not fall prey to intimidation. It is not just one of these virtues but the combination of all three that undergirds us. Paul would have listed only one if that was all it took. To walk in godly boldness, it takes all three.

We have already reviewed power and love in detail. Let's go on to attaining the mind of the Lord.

*A sound mind knows
what God is saying
and doing right now.*

Chapter 13

THE SPIRIT
OF A SOUND MIND

N othing intimidates more than ignorance."[1] Ignorance is a lack of knowledge. The value of knowledge is often spoken of in Scripture. Proverbs 24:5 says, "A wise man is strong, yes, a man of knowledge increases strength." And Proverbs 11:9 reminds us that "Through knowledge the righteous will be delivered." Knowledge gives the strength you need to escape intimidation's trap.

Realize that there is natural knowledge and spiritual knowledge. Spiritual knowledge and wisdom supersede natural knowledge and wisdom. That is why we call it *supernatural*. It is superior to the natural.

In 2 Timothy 1:6-7, Paul mentions to Timothy three key elements required to conquer fear (intimidation): love, power and a sound mind. This chapter covers the last element — the spirit of a sound mind.

What is a sound mind? Is it knowledge of the Scriptures? The disciples were considered ignorant fishermen, yet the most educated group in Israel, the Sanhedrin, was perplexed by their wisdom and boldness.

> Now when they saw the boldness of Peter and John, and perceived that they were uneducated and untrained men, they marveled. And they realized that they had been with Jesus (Acts 4:13).

A man named Stephen who waited tables for widows blew away the learned synagogue leaders. The Bible gives this account: "They were not able to resist the wisdom and the Spirit by which he spoke" (Acts 6:10).

Immediately we see that the spirit of a sound mind is not born of natural wisdom or special training in Scripture. So where does the spirit of a sound mind come from?

Revealed Knowledge

Soundness of mind comes by knowing the mind of Christ. Knowledge of Scripture alone is not knowing the mind of Christ. We are told that "the letter kills, but the Spirit gives life" (2 Cor. 3:6). The letter is the written Scriptures.

The Pharisees possessed great knowledge of the Scriptures without knowing the spirit of them; therefore, their ministry produced death. It pulled and pushed people away from the heart of God rather than drawing them to Him. They separated people from God with their legalistic knowledge, representing God as they perceived Him — with their heads and not their hearts.

Jesus declared, "Man shall not live by bread alone, but by every word that proceeds from the mouth of God" (Matt. 4:4). Notice He did not say "proceeded." That would be past tense. The Scriptures alone are what *proceeded* out of the mouth of God. He said "proceeds," which is present tense. We must know the Lord of the Scriptures to know what is *proceeding* out of His mouth today.

Jesus said in John 16:13-14, "However, when He, the Spirit of truth, has come, He will guide you into all truth; for He will not speak on His own authority, but whatever He hears He will speak; and He will tell you things to come. He will glorify Me, for He will take of what is Mine and declare it to you." Notice Jesus said, "whatever He hears," not "whatever He heard." With the help of the Holy Spirit, we can know what Jesus is saying.

You may ask then, "What good are the Scriptures?" They are guidelines to assist and direct us. They are God-breathed, and when quickened by the Holy Spirit they become alive in our hearts and not just in our heads. They are the standard we use to confirm that we have heard from the Spirit of God. The Holy Spirit will never speak contrary to the Scriptures. But we can get hung up when we limit what the Holy Spirit can say or do to that which fits into our mental understanding of the Scriptures. This was the error of the Pharisees.

Knowing Chapter and Verse Is Not Enough

The Pharisees were very knowledgeable. In fact, they memorized the first five books of the Old Testament! They had searched the Scriptures and were anxiously awaiting the Messiah. However, they watched for Him according to their mental understanding of the Scriptures. They knew Isaiah prophesied,

> For unto us a Child is born, unto us a Son is given; and the government will be upon His shoulder. And His name will be called Wonderful, Counselor, Mighty God, Everlasting Father, Prince of Peace. Of the increase of His government and peace There will be no end, upon the throne of David and over His kingdom, to order it and establish it with judgment and justice from that time forward, even forever. The zeal of the Lord of hosts will perform this (Is. 9:6-7).

Their Messiah would set up His earthly kingdom, deliver them from Roman oppression and be seated on the throne of David. So when Jesus came as a carpenter from Nazareth of Galilee, accompanied by disciples consisting of ignorant fishermen and tax collectors, they stumbled.

These Pharisees constantly confronted Jesus with issues they had invented from their mental understanding of the Scriptures. They were certain the Messiah would be a great national leader. So they confronted Jesus with questions such as, If you are the Messiah, where is the kingdom you are supposed to establish? Why are you not sitting on David's throne?

Jesus responded, "The kingdom of God does not come with observation; nor will they say, 'See here!' or 'See there!' For indeed, the kingdom of God is within you" (Luke 17:20-21). Now we may understand this today because we have the privilege of knowing that Jesus died and rose again, but these men truly believed they were right. However, they drew their confidence from their mental knowledge of Scripture. They did not have the Spirit's understanding.

Revealed by the Spirit

A man named Simeon was also looking for the Messiah. He was not as knowledgeable as the Pharisees. But look at what the Bible says about him.

> This man was just and devout, waiting for the Consolation of Israel, and the Holy Spirit was upon him. And it had been revealed to him by the Holy Spirit that he would not see death before he had seen the Lord's Christ. So he came by the Spirit into the temple. And when the parents brought in the Child Jesus, to do for Him according to the custom of the law, he took Him up in his arms and blessed God and said: "Lord, now You are letting Your servant depart in peace, according to Your word; for my eyes have seen Your salvation"...And Joseph and His mother marveled at those things which were spoken of Him (Luke 2:25-30,33).

When Jesus was brought to be dedicated to the Lord, He was anywhere from six months to two years old. The temple was huge; a number of buildings made up the temple area. There were usually hundreds, even thousands, of people in the area.

Now picture this: In comes a carpenter and his wife from Galilee carrying a six-month-old baby. They are in the midst of the crowd in the temple when this man, Simeon, runs over lifts up their baby and prophesies, "The Messiah!" You can understand why Joseph and Mary marveled!

Notice Simeon did not find out the Messiah was coming by reading a book titled *101 Reasons Why Messiah Will Come by 4 B.C.* He did not receive this information by studying the Scriptures. By the revelation of the Holy

Spirit he knew the Messiah was coming. He came to the temple under the direction and leading of the Holy Spirit!

Now here is an amazing fact to think about. This man, who was not an expert in the law, recognized Jesus as the Messiah when He was six months old, yet thirty years later the Pharisees could not recognize the Messiah as He cast out devils, healed the sick, opened blind eyes and raised the dead! That is the difference between having the mind of the Lord and having a mental knowledge of the Scriptures.

Could it be we have done with the New Testament what the Pharisees did with the Old? Have we limited our knowledge of God to our doctrine and our knowledge of the Scriptures, even in full gospel churches? Doctrine does not establish our relationship with God; it only defines it! When I said "I do" at my wedding, I did not get a manual! I began a personal relationship with my wife.

So should we stop reading our Bibles? Absolutely not! But perhaps we need to read them differently. When I pick up my Bible, I always pray, asking the Holy Spirit to reveal the Word of the Lord. As I read, truths explode within my heart. These truths are the word that I shall live by!

A sound mind knows what God is saying and doing right now. Only the Spirit of God can reveal this. He may communicate by Scripture; He may speak the word to my heart by an inward knowing or in His still, small voice. When we know what God is saying, we are founded on an unshakable rock.

He Speaks With Authority

The Gospels repeatedly relate how Jesus spoke with authority. Look at one such incident.

And so it was, when Jesus had ended these sayings, that the people were astonished at His teaching, for He taught them as one having authority, and not as the scribes (Matt. 7:28-29).

Not only did He speak with authority, but He also moved with authority. Look at another occasion.

Then they were all amazed and spoke among themselves, saying, "What a word this is! For with authority and power He commands the unclean spirits, and they come out" (Luke 4:36).

He lived and moved with such authority that it was recognized by a Roman centurion. He told Jesus that if He would only speak a word, his servant would be healed (Matt. 8:5-10). This Roman understood the source of Jesus' authority. Jesus' authority was not limited to Himself but was supplied by God. This was because Jesus was totally submitted to the Holy Spirit, who revealed His Father's will to Him.

The centurion said, "For I also am a man under authority, having soldiers under me". Jesus marveled when He heard this. This commander realized the only way to have authority is to be under authority! Jesus operated with authority because He was under authority. He was in complete submission to the Holy Spirit, who revealed the Father's will. He said:

For I have not spoken on My own authority; but the Father who sent Me gave Me a command, what I should say and what I should speak (John 12:49).

And again:

I can of Myself do nothing. As I hear, I judge;

and My judgment is righteous, because I do not seek My own will but the will of the Father who sent Me (John 5:30).

He explained clearly that His authority came from His Father.

Do you not believe that I am in the Father, and the Father in Me? The words that I speak to you I do not speak on My own authority; but the Father who dwells in Me does the works (John 14:10).

Most assuredly, I say to you, the Son can do nothing of Himself, but what He sees the Father do; for whatever He does, the Son also does in like manner (John 5:19).

Remember, even though He is the Son of God, He lived as a man filled with the Spirit of God. He stripped Himself of all divine privileges. Yet He commanded an authority that caused people to marvel. That's because He only spoke and acted as the Spirit of God led. He was never intimidated, because God is never afraid or intimidated. There is none more powerful, mighty and knowledgeable than God!

Jesus stayed in His authority even as the Pharisees continually tried to intimidate Him with their religious and crafty questions. They tried to trap Him in His own words, seeking to discredit Him. But no matter how clever their snare, He always answered by the Holy Spirit, breaking their intimidation. He confounded them with wisdom until in frustration they abandoned their attempts to intimidate Him.

And no one was able to answer Him a word, nor from that day on did anyone dare question Him anymore (Matt. 22:46).

As the Father Sent Me...

Now the exciting news: "As the Father has sent Me, I also send you" (John 20:21). We are to live, speak and move as He did. This is why He encourages us:

> Therefore settle it in your hearts not to meditate beforehand on what you will answer; for I will give you a mouth and wisdom which all your adversaries will not be able to contradict or resist (Luke 21:14-15).

The reason some do not speak, teach or preach with authority is because they study out a message from the Bible, then relate their mental understanding of these scriptures. They speak of what God said and did instead of what He is saying and doing! Only when we speak by the Spirit of God will we speak with authority.

> For He Himself has said, "I will never leave you nor forsake you." So we may boldly say: "The Lord is my helper; I will not fear. What can man do to me?" (Heb. 13:5-6).

Look carefully at those words again. We can speak with boldness and authority when we know what He is saying! The surety of His word gives us boldness. God has assured us that when we know what He says, and when we believe He is always with us, we can boldly declare, "What can man do to me?" When we live in this confidence, we cannot be intimidated!

Modern-day Pharisees

On occasion I have been approached by those I call modern-day Pharisees who do not have the Spirit. (They may claim to speak in tongues, but they still do not have the Spirit of God!) They quote chapter and verse faster than most.

These people have confronted me with questions about what I had just preached or perhaps something I had written. I am not referring to people who ask questions in order to learn or because they don't understand. I welcome these. No, I am talking about those who run everything through their own religious parameters, rejecting anyone or anything that doesn't fit into their doctrinal box.

I have noticed that the conversation can go one of two directions. First, I can get into a mental discussion of Scripture with them and wear myself out, especially if they are very well versed on the point they are trying to make. They will prevail, and I will be intimidated. I have learned not to get caught up in this!

The other way to respond is to look to the Holy Spirit and speak what I hear in my heart. Then the wisdom of God comes forth, and their arguments cease. The wisdom of God will always be from the Scriptures, but it has life breathed into it by the Holy Spirit.

Years ago I was with another minister on an airplane. We met a Jewish woman who was very outgoing and witty. We got into an intense conversation with her about the Lord Jesus. We fired statements back and forth to one another, attempting to prove Jesus as the Messiah. All the while she was attempting to prove His claims to be false.

All of a sudden I realized what I was doing. I knew this mental discussion would go nowhere. So I looked within for the Holy Spirit's guidance, and He revealed what I should speak. I looked at her and shared the words He gave me. As I did, my voice changed, and an authority came on what I was saying. As soon as she heard these words, her eyes got big, and she was silent. All our debating had not helped her. But when the word of the Lord came, she was immediately ministered to.

After we got off the plane, the minister I was traveling with said, "John, I could sense the presence of the Lord when you spoke those words. Did you notice she had nothing more to say?" Don't get caught up in fruitless discussions ruled by mental understanding of the Scriptures. Instead, let the Holy Spirit guide you into spiritual wisdom.

> These things we also speak, not in words which man's wisdom teaches but which the Holy Spirit teaches, comparing spiritual things with spiritual...He who is spiritual judges all things, yet he himself is rightly judged by no one. For "who has known the mind of the Lord that he may instruct Him?" But we have the mind of Christ (1 Cor. 2:13,15-16).

The man who has the mind of Christ cannot be judged or intimidated! I could share numerous incidents when I would have been intimidated if I had not looked to the Spirit of God.

We are admonished to walk as Jesus walked (1 John 2:6). Jesus only did what He saw the Holy Spirit do. If we do that, we will have soundness of mind and possess the boldness we need to overcome intimidation and control.

Lord, What Am I to Do?

Often we face situations that would paralyze us, rendering us unable to complete what God has set before us, if we did not have the mind of Christ. I faced one such challenge in Mexico.

I was invited to Monterey, Mexico, for a citywide evangelistic meeting. It was only for one evening, and I paid the expenses to go there. I spent half the day in prayer. As I prayed, I saw a dark cloud over the building where we were to meet. I asked the Lord what it was. He explained

181

"John, that is the darkness that is fighting against this meeting. Continue to pray."

A very strong anointing came on me, strengthening me to pray. Within thirty minutes I saw something else. A shaft of light went from the top of the building straight up to the sky. Again, I asked the Lord what it was. "That is my unhindered glory coming in the meeting tonight," He said to my spirit. I was so excited.

The service was scheduled to begin at 6:00 p.m. We arrived a little early, only to be greeted with the news that a government official wanted to see the pastor who organized the meeting. This government official was accompanied by two uniformed officers.

The pastor and I went to meet with the official. He spoke for awhile to the pastor in Spanish, then turned and questioned me in English. "Do you speak Spanish?"

"No, sir," I answered.

He then ordered me, "You will say nothing to this crowd tonight except about tourist-related activities."

Then he turned back to the pastor and spoke with him. I watched the pastor. He did not look very happy. In fact, he looked quite scared.

When the official finished, he and the two soldiers left. The pastor pulled me aside and said, "John, this man is a government official, and he says you cannot preach. There is a law in Mexico that you cannot preach in this country without a permit if you are not a citizen." He went on to say, "It is a law that usually is not enforced, but this guy obviously does not want you here, and he is exercising it. He also said he wants you in his office at nine o'clock Monday morning."

I could not believe what my ears were hearing. I immediately said to the pastor, "Look, I didn't fly all the way down here not to preach. If you are concerned only for me, then let me preach."

The pastor said, "John, it could also affect my church. He could cause a lot of problems. He is a high-ranking official. We had better not let you preach." This pastor was intimidated, and I could do nothing but pray, because he was in authority over that meeting.

I went outside the building, a gymnasium located in downtown Monterey. There was a flagpole in front, and I began to walk around it. I knew God had shown me in prayer His glory manifested in this service. I knew God had instructed me to come. But I didn't know what to do now. The thought kept running through my mind, Would this intimidating official keep me from what God had sent me to do? Then I'd reason, This man cannot stop what God has shown me in prayer. Back and forth I wrestled, What do I do?

I then said, "Father, I don't know what to do, but You're not surprised by this. You already knew this would happen. So I need Your wisdom and counsel for this situation." I began to pray in the Spirit. This scripture came to my mind.

> Counsel in the heart of man is like deep water, but a man of understanding will draw it out (Prov. 20:5).

Jesus said that believers would have rivers of living water flowing out of their hearts (John 7:38). I needed the river of the counsel of God. I needed the mind of Christ. Praying in tongues would bring it forth.

After praying for several minutes, my mind was quieted enough to hear more. This thought bubbled up from my heart: Tell the people about the greatest tourist to ever visit Mexico.

I shouted out loud, "That's it! The man said I could talk about tourism. I will tell them about the greatest tourist to ever come to Mexico — Jesus Christ!" Joy rose up within me, and I began to laugh.

I ran back into the building. To my delight God had already dealt with the pastor. He said, "God spoke to me and told me to tell you to do whatever He says."

I opened the service by saying, "I was told only to talk to you about tourist-related activities. So tonight I want to tell you about the greatest tourist to ever come to Mexico."

I preached Jesus as Lord and Savior for an hour. Several responded to the call to receive Jesus Christ as Lord. There was a disabled man in this group. After I prayed for those in the group to receive Jesus, the Lord spoke to me, "There is the first man I want to heal."

I looked at him and said, "Sir, the Spirit of God says He wants to heal you." I laid hands on him and prayed. Then I took him by the hand, and we began to walk. He was very cautious at first. Then he moved faster and faster. Soon he was walking; then we ran together. Finally, I let go of his hand, and he ran by himself.

The crowd went wild. People with all manner of sickness and disease ran to the front. In all the confusion I lost my interpreter. A couple of hundred people had stormed toward the stage. Many were healed, including one woman who had been totally deaf in one ear since birth and partially deaf in the other. She wept until her blouse was soaked with her tears. It was wonderful!

I was unaware that the government official had sent two men back to the meeting to arrest me if I preached. They arrived just as I was praying for the disabled man. An usher spotted them and heard them say, "Let's watch what he does before we arrest him."

When they saw the disabled man healed, one asked the other, "Do you think this is real?" They moved closer and continued to watch what God was doing.

When they saw the deaf woman healed and weeping, one said, "I think this is real."

Then a five-year-old boy fell on the floor, obviously under the power of God. Seeing this, they agreed: This is real! And these two men who were sent to arrest me came forward for prayer! Hallelujah!

I left the country the next day, and I didn't bother keeping the appointment with the official. The next week the Mexican pastor flew to the United States, bringing along a copy of the Monterey newspaper. He read me an article in the front section about our meeting.

The newspaper reported that the government officials said I was a fraud, and all I wanted was money. (I had been led not to take a penny out of the country and had covered my own expenses. After hearing this, I knew why.) However, the newspaper went on to state that its own reporters saw people genuinely getting healed! Glory be to God!

The government official attempted to stop me with his intimidating threats. If the pastor and I had come under the control of those threats, the gift of God in our lives would have been dormant. No one would have been saved or ministered to that evening. God's word, which He spoke to me by His Spirit, had given me boldness to break through the intimidation released against me. That's the power of a sound mind.

*What man considers
insignificant
God uses to perform
the impossible.*

Chapter 14

Press On

Nehemiah was a Jew who lived at the time when Israel was in captivity. Several years before, Babylonians had come and utterly destroyed Jerusalem. They killed or took captive most of its inhabitants. The walls were burned and broken down, the city left in ruins.

God had put it in Nehemiah's heart to return to Jerusalem and rebuild the walls and the city. Nehemiah had served the foreign king faithfully and had won favor with him. The king granted him permission to leave and fulfill all God had put in his heart. Nehemiah immediately departed for Jerusalem and gathered the remnant of Israel, encouraging them to restore all that the enemy had destroyed.

They were up against tremendous resistance. Three local officials named Sanballat, Tobiah and Geshem did not want the walls rebuilt. They opposed the prosperity of Israel. They were determined to stop Nehemiah and God's remnant, and they hatched all kinds of plots to intimidate them.

When these leaders first learned of his plans, Nehemiah reported, "They laughed at us and despised us" (Neh. 2:19). Not only did they try to discourage Nehemiah and his men, but they also tried to make them look foolish in the eyes of the people. They mocked them with belittling statements. "Whatever they build, if even a fox goes up on it, he will break down their stone wall" (Neh. 4:3).

Often people try to intimidate you by laughing at you or making light of what you are doing. They may mock you and question your ability to perform all that God has put in your heart. They might do this to your face, or they might sow questions and mockery among others. Or perhaps it is not a person or group that resists you, but you wrestle with your own mind as it is bombarded with thoughts such as, What will people think? Will they laugh at me? Will I fail?

In this situation it is important that we know what God has instructed us to do, remembering that He "has chosen the weak things of the world to put to shame the things which are mighty" (1 Cor. 1:27). What man considers insignificant, God uses to perform the impossible. Then He gets all the glory!

Nehemiah fasted and prayed until he had the mind of the Lord. He then could boldly refute his adversaries. "The God of heaven Himself will prosper us; therefore we His servants will arise and build, but you have no heritage or right of memorial in Jerusalem" (Neh. 2:20).

When they realized they couldn't stop Nehemiah, and the Israelites were progressing in their work, they became enraged. They were no longer laughing, because it was no longer funny. They plotted to throw the whole project into confusion by attacking the city (Neh. 4:7-8).

Anger is another weapon of intimidation. It will be wielded against you in order to stop or deter you. From this anger can come blatant — or subtle — threats. This distraction is a very effective tool of intimidation. I have watched many times as people backed away from what they knew was right or what they should do, in order to avoid the wrath of others. They made special concessions in order to keep a false peace.

Pressure Without and Within

Not only did Nehemiah have to face this attack from ungodly outsiders, but he also had problems arising among his own men concerning the conditions they all faced. Often when God commissions us, we face resistance and opposition from without and within.

Nehemiah's men had become weary. They were facing so much rubbish that it was hindering their progress (Neh. 4:10). There was another problem as well. His wealthy workers put financial pressure on the families who were in debt, charging them large sums of interest on the fields they farmed (Neh. 5:1-8). This discouraged the men whose families were suffering. These internal problems made it even harder to resist the coercion and discouragement from their enemy.

Intimidation on Every Side

I have been in situations like this. When I first began traveling, I was asked to help a church that had lost its pastor. It was in a small town of eight hundred people in the middle of nowhere. After two services every teenager there had repented and experienced the power of God, as had many adults. Because of what God was doing, the attendance doubled to almost one hundred. My wife and I felt such compassion for these people that we offered to cancel our next six weeks of meetings and stay to build a strong foundation in this church to prepare it for a new pastor.

Some people on the board didn't like what I preached. One man was upset because when he came into the third service, all the teenagers were sitting on the front two rows of the church where he and his wife normally sat. Previously, these young men and women had sat in the very back of the church.

Others felt I ministered too strongly. The bottom line was that the men on the board wanted to control me. They wanted to run the church their way. After several meetings with them I finally said, "I will be the one in authority for the six weeks I am here, and then your new pastor will take over. This is the only way it will work. You decide."

The day they were to give me their decision I had a call from a local drug pusher whose wife was attending the meetings. She had confessed to him she was committing adultery with his best friend. He decided to take his frustration out on me and the church. He told me he was going to cause trouble that night.

I didn't pay much attention to his threat. A few hours later one of the board members who was supportive of us informed me this man had called him and threatened to bomb the meeting. I told the board member, "Call the police and ask them to look into it."

A few hours later I received a call from the police. An officer said, "Mr. Bevere, please come down to the station and sign this document to get a warrant for this man's arrest."

I said, "Officer, I don't want to see this man arrested. He is hurting. All I am asking for is a little protection tonight outside the building."

He said, "My shift ends in four hours, and the nearest

police station is thirty-five miles away. They won't be able to send anyone tonight."

I answered, "I still don't want the man arrested."

The officer questioned me: "Mr. Bevere, how long have you lived here?"

I told him I didn't live in that town.

He said, "Mr. Bevere, I know this man. He has a reputation in these parts. He is a suspected drug runner. If he has a few beers, I wouldn't put anything past him."

I couldn't believe what I was hearing. The police were saying this man was dangerous, so I knew he must really be. But I still felt no release to sign the warrant request. So I refused, then thanked the officer.

I was not only dealing with this man's threats but also the problems with the board. I thought, This is ridiculous. This board is giving me a hard time. They don't want me here. Now my family and I are being threatened by a madman.

Everything in me wanted to shake the dust off my feet and get my family out of town before sundown. If I had not known God had sent me, I would have left for the sake of my family. However, my heart wouldn't allow me to go for three reasons: First, God had sent me, and I hadn't heard Him tell me to leave. Second, I did not want to abandon all those who had been touched. And third, if you run once because of intimidation, it is easier to run the next time.

I had the mind of the Lord and decided to stay, if that was what the board agreed to. I prayed all that afternoon. It was one of the strongest times of prayer I have ever had. The gift of God was strengthened in me. I was ready for the evening.

But when I got to the church, I learned that I would not be staying. The board had met just before the service was to start. One of the deacons informed me that they had voted that I should leave. The service that night would be my last.

I was grieved, but I determined to focus simply on what God wanted to do for the people that night. I preached a powerful message, and the power of God hit so strongly that people were all over the floor. Many who were backslidden gave their lives to the Lord. The man who made the threat didn't even show up. At the end of the service I had to announce that the board did not want me to stay. An outcry went up among the people. I had not come to bring division, so I felt at peace about leaving.

A week later that same board elected a pastor who was later discovered to be a homosexual. They went through four pastors in the next year. The spirit of intimidation that was at work in that church board caused serious destruction to that congregation.

Stay Strong and Focused

No sooner had Nehemiah dealt with the internal struggles among his men than another wave of intimidation hit.

> Sanballat and Geshem sent to me, saying, "Come, let us meet together among the villages in the plain of Ono." But they thought to do me harm. So I sent messengers to them, saying, "I am doing a great work, so that I cannot come down. Why should the work cease while I leave it and go down to you?" But they sent me this message four times, and I answered them in the same manner (Neh. 6:2-4).

Sanballat and Geshem persisted, trying to distract Nehemiah. But Nehemiah stayed strong, focusing on what God had commanded him to do. He would not be deterred from his commission.

The enemy wants to sidetrack us to make us ineffective

in our labor. Satan will not try this only once. He is persistent. We must be stronger in our resolve than he is in his. That is why the Bible says we are to "resist him, steadfast in the faith" (1 Pet. 5:9). The word *steadfast* means "strong, firm and immovable." Too many people give up after a few hits from the enemy rather than remaining immovable until the victory is complete.

Sanballat sent his servant a fifth time to Nehemiah, this time with a letter that accused him of being in rebellion and setting himself up as king of Judah (Neh. 6:5-7). This was a blatant lie.

Nehemiah still would not stop. He was too focused to be sidetracked by slander. Too often we are drawn off course by trying to smooth things over with an enemy who is trying to intimidate us.

I have had to look at people and say, "Why are you allowing the lies of this person to affect what God has called you to do? Just because he accuses you doesn't mean he is right or he wants the truth! You need to know what God says about you and His plan for you. Why try to reason with foolishness?" The Bible says, "Do not answer a fool according to his folly, lest you also be like him" (Prov. 26:4).

The last person who attempted to stop Nehemiah was a man who came and prophesied that he should seek refuge in the temple, because the enemy was coming to kill him (Neh. 6:10). But if Nehemiah left the work site, it would weaken the men and keep the work from completion.

Nehemiah responded, "Should such a man as I flee? And who is there such as I who would go into the temple to save his life? I will not go in!" (Neh. 6:11). Nehemiah then perceived that God had not sent this man at all: he pronounced this prophecy against Nehemiah because Tobiah and Sanballat had hired him. Now look at what Nehemiah said after this:

He had been hired to intimidate me so that I would commit a sin by doing this, and then they would give me a bad name to discredit me (Neh. 6:13, NIV).

The enemy can give you a bad name by intimidating you into protecting yourself at all costs. Nehemiah had the mind of the Lord; therefore, he was able to discern the pure and true from the evil and deceptive.

Nehemiah summed up the schemes of Sanballat, Geshem and Tobiah as follows:

For they all were trying to make us afraid, saying, "Their hands will be weakened in the work, and it will not be done." Now therefore, O God, strengthen my hands (Neh. 6:9).

Again we see the purpose of intimidation: to weaken us so we cannot accomplish the will of God and will no longer resist the intimidator. If we do not stand against this steadfastly, we will succumb.

Our enemy the devil attempts many different avenues of intimidation when we invade his territory. He doesn't try once and then give up. If he can stop, postpone or weaken us, then he keeps the kingdom of God from advancing.

Nehemiah and his men did finish the wall. Now surrounded by protection, the city was on its way to restoration. It was not easy. Tremendous resistance and opposition met them every step of the way. But the people knew God had spoken, and they refused to back off.

Breaking Through Resistance

Nehemiah's tenacity is a classic example of what believers are exhorted to do:

> Not that I have already attained, or am already
> perfected; but I press on, that I may lay hold
> of that for which Christ Jesus has also laid hold
> of me (Phil. 3:12).

The key word is *press*. If Paul said by the Holy Spirit, "I press on," then, as with Nehemiah, he worked through frequent resistance. We don't just stumble onto it. We must press into it. Paul went on to say,

> I press toward the mark for the prize of the high
> calling of God in Christ Jesus (Phil. 3:14, KJV).

There is a high calling and a low calling. The high calling is a life lived on earth according to heaven's standards; it is see the kingdom of God manifested through an individual life. People who live in the high calling control their surroundings. By staying in their authority, they change the spiritual climate from oppression to liberty.

Darkness cannot overpower light. Light expels darkness. The brighter the light, the more the darkness is displaced. This is how it is when we walk in the authority of God's kingdom. We place our surroundings under its rule.

Jesus could eat with sinners because He controlled the atmosphere. If you are stronger in God than the unbeliever is in the devil, you will control the atmosphere. If a sinner is more dominant in evil than the believer is in righteousness, the unbeliever will control the spiritual climate.

When you decide to live in the high call, you will face opposition and resistance. "Yes, and all who desire to live godly in Christ Jesus will suffer persecution" (2 Tim. 3:12). Again we are told, "We must through many tribulations enter the kingdom of God" (Acts 14:22).

Yet many Christians settle for and live in the low calling. Why? They do not want to face the resistance that accompanies pressing toward the high calling. They would rather conform to their surroundings than change them by godly confrontation. It is much easier to blend in than stand out. When faced with opposition, some settle for compromise and seek the path of least resistance.

I believe our unwillingness to resist may be partly attributed to the ease and security we build into our lives. We carefully design our lifestyles in order to avoid any form of hardship. Not that I advocate voluntary hardship, but I do believe that we trust our plans and programs more than we trust God.

We have insurance. If we get sick, we rush to the doctor without praying first, knowing our insurance will cover the cost. Our jobs provide a paycheck every week or two. If we lose our job, we have unemployment to fall back on. If that runs out, there is welfare. If welfare is unavailable, we may be able to find another program that will take care of us — maybe even one that compensates laziness.

Television further encourages our passive lifestyle. The average American watches about twenty-four hours of television a week![1] We allow the networks and Hollywood to think for us. Our ideas are formed by what we absorb from their programming.

Microwave ovens and fast-food chains promise us instant food with little or no labor. Some even guarantee a free meal if the food is not served within fifteen minutes. We have overnight mail, one-hour dry cleaning, one-hour photo processing, quick lube for cars and access to world news around the clock — and these are just a few of the conveniences available to us.

Most of these are fine; they should free us to pursue what is really important. However, we often fail to choose what is important. Too many people today will not pursue something if they have to work hard for it.

Unfortunately, this mentality has infiltrated our Western

church. Few Christians possess the persistently determined character necessary to obtain the high calling of God. When met with opposition, they turn aside to the path of least resistance. At first this escape route appears to be a good choice, with its promise of ease. But this road is paved with the characteristics of lukewarmness: compromise, apathy and self-preservation.

Jesus instructed us to confront the mountains of adversity, then they will be removed. To paraphrase: Blast the mountain, even if you have to do it stone by stone! Like Nehemiah, true warriors in Christ press through the mountains, confident that nothing is impossible to those who believe (Matt. 17:20). In contrast, those traveling the path of ease go around their mountains to avoid confrontation.

The flow to the world's system is set by the prince of the power of the air (Eph. 2:2). Heaven's domain is in direct opposition to this flow. To go heaven's way means we will constantly face confrontation from this world's system. Unfortunately, this worldly system is prevalent in our churches as well.

I compare this opposition to rowing a boat against the current of a fast-flowing river. You have to continually press against the flow of the water. Your oars must be firmly placed in the water, and you must continue to row. You cannot let up for one moment. If you do, you may continue to move upstream a short way because of existing momentum, but it won't be long before you are heading down the river. Your boat may still point upstream, but you are heading downstream. This illustrates what happens when believers do not press on. They still point in the direction of Christianity, but they are now flowing backward with the world. They become religious. They lose their power and are ineffective. To quote the exact words of Jesus, they are "good for nothing" (Matt. 5:13)!

Be Strong!

After Paul exhorted Timothy to stir up the gift of God, he quickly added, "You therefore, my son, be strong in the grace that is in Christ Jesus" (2 Tim. 2:1). To press forward and overcome intimidation we must be strong.

Likewise Paul admonished the church at Corinth, "Watch, stand fast in the faith, be brave, be strong" (1 Cor. 16:13). A brave believer faces difficult situations without shrinking from them.

God encouraged Joshua not once, but seven times, to be strong and of good courage!

> Only be strong and very courageous, that you may observe to do according to all the law which Moses My servant commanded you; do not turn from it to the right hand or to the left, that you may prosper wherever you go (Josh. 1:7).

Notice God said to be strong and very courageous. For what purpose? To win wars or be a great leader? No, for the purpose of keeping the Word of the Lord. By this Joshua would be a great leader and win every war! Intimidation attempts to strip you of your freedom to obey the will or word of God. Therefore, we must be strong and courageous at all times lest we unknowingly drift away from what we know to be right.

Let's define the word *courage:*

> The attitude or response of facing and dealing with anything recognized as difficult, dangerous or painful instead of withdrawing from it.[2]

Now what is the opposite of courage? You might automatically assume the opposite to be fear or weakness. And this is true to an extent. However, let's add the prefix *dis*. We get the word *discourage*. So God commanded Joshua, and us, to be strong and brave, not allowing discouragement into our hearts. Discouragement will keep us from fulfilling His will!

Let's define *discourage:*

> To deprive of courage; make less confident or hopeful; dishearten.[3]

Remember how Elijah was overwhelmed with discouragement because of Jezebel's intimidation? He withdrew and ran. He was so disheartened that he was knocked out of his authority. We need to treat discouragement as an enemy. We underestimate its power to prevent us from obtaining the high calling of God. If God tells Joshua seven times to be strong and courageous, then we must take heed also. Discouragement is a killer! If not confronted, it will cause us to draw back.

> Now the just shall live by faith; but if anyone draws back, My soul has no pleasure in him (Heb. 10:38).

It is important to realize that God takes no pleasure in cowards. We are told, "He who overcomes shall inherit all things, and I will be his God and he shall be My son. But the *cowardly*, unbelieving, abominable, murderers, sexually immoral, sorcerers, idolaters, and all liars shall have their part in the lake which burns with fire and brimstone, which is the second death" (Rev. 21:7-8, italics added).

The word *coward* means "one who shows ignoble fear in the face of pain or danger."[4] Isn't it sobering that God groups cowards with murderers and the sexually immoral? Yet we excuse ourselves, claiming that cowardly behavior is a weakness.

No, cowardice comes from unbelief. And unbelief cost

the children of Israel their lives. They never entered their promised land. "So we see that they could not enter in because of unbelief" (Heb. 3:19).

It is no different today. A coward does not conquer. He will not receive that which is promised. The Lord strongly exhorted us through the apostle Paul:

> Only let your conduct be worthy of the gospel of Christ, so that whether I come and see you or am absent, I may hear of your affairs, that you stand fast...and not in any way terrified by your adversaries (Phil. 1:27-28).

Stand fast and don't allow your adversaries to terrify you. Be brave, strong and courageous, ready to face and deal with any opposition rather than withdrawing from it! In the very next verse Paul continues:

> For to you it has been granted on behalf of Christ, not only to believe in Him, but also to suffer for His sake (Phil. 1:29).

What is this suffering we are to experience? Peter answers with:

> Therefore, since Christ suffered for us in the flesh, arm yourselves also with the same mind, for he who has suffered in the flesh has ceased from sin, that he no longer should live the rest of his time in the flesh for the lusts [desires] of men, but for the will of God (1 Pet. 4:1-2).

The suffering we face and endure comes when our own flesh or the influence of others pressures us to go one direction while the will of God for us is to go in the opposite direction. We are commanded to be strong and courageous so that we might keep the word of the Lord.

Peter said we should arm ourselves for this. A Christian who is not armed or prepared to suffer is like a soldier who goes to battle unarmed. This soldier will either be captured or killed. Christians who are not armed to suffer are easily captured and held imprisoned by the fear of man — intimidation.

We should expect to encounter the resistance that accompanies our pursuit of the high calling; however, Paul was quick to say confidently, "The Lord will deliver me from every evil work and preserve me for His heavenly kingdom. To Him be glory forever and ever. Amen!" (2 Tim. 4:18). God will always deliver us to His glory. Hallelujah!

Carefully read the following exhortations from God's Word. Read them as if you had never seen them before. Stop and take the time to meditate carefully on each word, allowing the Holy Spirit to illuminate them.

> If God is for us [me], who can be against us [me]? (Rom. 8:31).

> Who shall separate us from the love of Christ? Shall tribulation, or distress, or persecution, or famine, or nakedness, or peril, or sword?...Yet in all these things we are more than conquerors through Him who loved us (Rom. 8:35,37).

> You are of God, little children, and have overcome them, because He who is in you is greater than he who is in the world (1 John 4:4).

Guard the purity of your heart and stay in your position of authority as God's child and servant. Then you can boldly declare:

> *The Lord is my helper; I will not fear.*
> *What can man do to me?*

201

In closing I exhort you never to allow any previous failures to hold you back. Don't judge your future by where you've been! If you do, you'll never go beyond your past! No matter how often you have fallen, there is unfailing hope — God specializes in turning cowards into champions! Hallelujah! His power is perfected in weakness.

As an example of encouragement look at the life of Andrew, Simon Peter's brother. The night Jesus was arrested, "All the disciples forsook Him and fled" (Matt. 26:56). Peter wasn't the only one who was intimidated; Andrew had fled for his life too. Yet this one act of cowardice didn't mean Andrew would remain a coward.

After the resurrection of Jesus, Andrew preached in

Ethiopia, which was under Roman rule. The following is an historical account of how he glorified Jesus.

When Andrew, through his diligent preaching, had brought many to the faith of Christ, Aegeas the governor asked permission of the Roman senate to force all Christians to sacrifice to and honor the Roman idols. Andrew thought he should resist Aegeas and went to him, telling him that a judge of men should first know and worship his Judge in heaven. While worshipping the true God, Andrew said, he should banish all false gods and blind idols from his mind.

Furious at Andrew, Aegeas demanded to know if he was the man who had recently overthrown the temple of the gods and persuaded men to become Christians — a "superstitious sect" that had recently been declared illegal by the Romans.

Andrew replied that the rulers of Rome didn't understand the truth. The Son of God, who came into the world for man's sake, taught that the Roman gods were devils, enemies of mankind, teaching men to offend God and causing Him to turn away from them. By serving the devil, men fall into all kinds of wickedness, Andrew said, and after they die, nothing but their evil deeds are remembered.

The proconsul ordered Andrew not to preach these things any more or he would face a speedy crucifixion. Whereupon Andrew replied, "I would not have preached the honor and glory of the cross if I feared the death of the cross." He was condemned to be crucified for teaching a new sect and taking away the religion of the Roman gods.

Andrew, going toward the place of execution and seeing the cross waiting for him, never changed his expression. Neither did he fail in his speech. His body fainted not, nor did his reason fail him, as often happens to men about to die. He said, "O cross, most welcomed and longed for! With a willing mind, joyfully and desirously, I come to you, being the scholar of Him which did hang on you, because I have always been your lover and yearned to embrace you."[1]

This was not the same man who ran for his life when Jesus was arrested. He had changed.

In fact all the disciples who had fled were eventually killed for their testimony of Jesus Christ. God granted them the privilege of facing the very thing they ran from. In laying down their own lives, intimidation's power was broken!

This should comfort you, knowing "that He who has begun a good work in you will complete it until the day of Jesus Christ" (Phil. 1:6). The testimony of these disciples bears witness to how God turns our failures into victory! Don't draw back, but dare to believe the One who loved you and gave Himself for you.

Let's pray together:

Father, in the name of Jesus I ask You to strengthen me through Your love and wisdom. Forgive me for drawing back in times of difficulty in order to preserve my own comfort and security. Lord Jesus, this day I choose to deny myself, take up my cross and follow You. I am Your servant; I receive Your grace that empowers so I might speak Your word and perform Your will with all boldness and love.

Now address the spirit of fear and control:

> I break the words of intimidation and control spoken over my life by myself or others. I break the grip of the fear of man off my life. You unclean spirits of darkness, I submit myself to God and I resist you. I will give you no place in my life, so go in the name of my Lord Jesus Christ. Amen.

Now to Him who is able to keep you from
stumbling, and to present you faultless
before the presence of His glory with exceeding joy,
to God our Savior, Who alone is wise,
be glory and majesty, dominion and power,
both now and forever. Amen.

Jude 24-25

Notes

Chapter 5
Dormant Gifts

1. A letter from Edmund Burke to William Smith, 9 January 1795.
2. The Oxford English Dictionary.
3. Merriam-Webster's Collegiate Dictionary, 10th edition.
4. The Oxford English Dictionary.

Chapter 8
Stir the Gift

1. Tyndale, *New Bible Dictionary,* 2nd edition.

Chapter 9
The Root of Intimidation

1. Logos Bible software, version 1.6 (Oak Harbor, Wash.: Logos Research Systems Inc., 1993).
2. "Day of judgment" here refers to judgment hurled against a believer by wicked men. See Romans 3:4 and Is. 54:17.

Chapter 13
The Spirit of a Sound Mind

1. H. Lawrence, 1646.

Chapter 14
Press On

1. Statistical Abstracts, 1994.
2. Merriam-Webster's Collegiate Dictionary, 10th edition.
3. Ibid.
4. Ibid.

Epilogue

1. John Foxe, *Foxe's Christian Martyrs of the World* (Greensburg, Pa.: Barbour and Company Inc., 1991), pp. 6-7.

Strong, James. *The New Strong's Exhaustive Concordance of the BIble*. Nashville, Tenn.: Thomas Nelson, 1984.

Vine, W.E., Merrill F. Unger and William White, Jr. *An Expository Dictionary of Biblical Words*. Nashville, Tenn.: Thomas Nelson, 1984

OTHER BOOKS BY JOHN BEVERE

The Bait of Satan
Your Response Determines Your Future

Have you been trapped? This book exposes one of Satan's most deceptive snares that he uses to pull believers out of the will of God — the snare of offense. It is crucial that everyone is aware of this trap. Jesus said, "It is impossible that offenses will not come" (Luke 17:1). The question is not, Will you encounter the bait of Satan? Rather, How will you respond? Don't let another's sin or mistake affect your relationship with God!

Victory in the Wilderness
Growing Strong in Dry Times

"God! Where are you?" Do you wonder if you've missed God or somehow displeased Him? More than likely this is not the case — instead you have arrived in the wilderness. You're not experiencing God's rejection but your season of preparation for a fresh move of God.

Some issues addressed in this book: • How God refines • Why spiritual dry times? • Is the wilderness necessary? • What it takes to make a champion of God.

The Voice of One Crying
A Prophetic Message for Today!

What is a prophet's reward? God is restoring the prophetic office to turn the hearts of His people to Him. Yet, this office is often reduced to predictions of the future by a word of knowledge or wisdom rather than a declaration of the church's true condition and destiny. Many, fed up with hype and superficial ministry, are ready to receive the true prophetic message.

Some issues addressed in this book: • Message of the true prophetic • The Elijah anointing • Recognizing false prophets • Idolatry in America • Exposing deception.

AUDIOVISUAL MATERIALS BY JOHN BEVERE

Video Cassette Messages by John Bevere

Baptism of Fire
The Bait of Satan
Breaking Intimidation
Does God Know You?

Can You Walk Free
from Sin?
The Coming Glory

Other titles available

Audio Cassette Messages by John Bevere

Walking with God
Pursue the High Call
Breaking through
Resistance
Armed to Suffer

The Wilderness
Birthing in the Spirit
Standing Strong
Overcoming Offenses

Other titles available

To request our free newsletter and a catalog
of available materials, or to obtain information
on having John or Lisa Bevere minister in your
community, please use the following address:

John Bevere Ministries
P.O. Box 2002
Apopka, Florida 32704-2002
Phone: (407) 889-9617
Fax: (407) 889-2065